CAREERS NEW AND UNIQUE

Some people want a career that is different from the usual work that most people do. Today there are a number of new careers developing as varied as nuclear-medicine specialists, demographers, and horticulturists. In this book the author has gathered together all the information needed to make a career decision and plan an appropriate education that will lead to an unusual occupation.

OTHER BOOKS BY SARAH SPLAVER

CAREER CHOICES IN PSYCHOLOGY
NONTRADITIONAL CAREERS FOR WOMEN
NONTRADITIONAL COLLEGE ROUTES TO CAREERS
PARAPROFESSIONS:
    CAREERS OF THE FUTURE AND THE PRESENT
YOUR CAREER—IF YOU'RE NOT GOING TO COLLEGE
YOUR HANDICAP—DON'T LET IT HANDICAP YOU
YOUR PERSONALITY AND YOUR CAREER

CAREERS NEW AND UNIQUE

By SARAH SPLAVER, Ph.D.

Julian Messner  New York

Copyright © 1979 by Sarah Splaver
All rights reserved including the right of
reproduction in whole or in part in any form.
Published by Julian Messner, a Simon & Schuster
Division of Gulf & Western Corporation, Simon &
Schuster Building, 1230 Avenue of the Americas,
New York, N.Y. 10020.

JULIAN MESSNER and colophon are trademarks of Simon
& Schuster, registered in the U.S. Patent and Trade-
mark Office.

Manufactured in the United States of America

Second Printing, 1981

Design by Miriam Temple

Library of Congress Cataloging in Publication Data

Splaver, Sarah.
    Careers new and unique.

    Bibliography: p.
    Includes index.
    SUMMARY: Provides information needed to make a
career decision and plan an appropriate education that
will lead to an unusual occupation. Among the careers
discussed are those of radiographer, aerospace scientist,
tape librarian, and inhalation therapist.
    1. Vocational guidance—Juvenile literature.
[1. Vocational guidance]   1. Title.
HF5381.2.S58   331′.7′02   79–20032
ISBN 0-671-32938-3

To Adam, Joey, Michael Frederick, and
Michael Jay
may their futures be bright and happy in new
and unique careers.

CONTENTS

CONTENTS

Contents

CONTENTS

1

You Seek the New and Unique

The lives of American workers have changed almost incredibly from the start of the twentieth century to our present approach to the end of this century. Improved working conditions, shorter workweeks, better opportunities for workers who wish to advance or change positions, higher wages, and increased employee benefits of all sorts have made the lot of the American worker much better than it ever was.

Additionally, new and/or unique career opportunities have arisen. In transportation, for example, we have come a long way from the horse and buggy of 1900 to the horseless carriage to our present-day automobiles to jet airplanes to our superspaceships that go to the moon. Many advances and changes have taken place, especially in science and technology, resulting in new industries and new fields of employment, and also in new positions in older professions and long-established fields.

You may be among the many thousands of young people—and older ones—who are eagerly seeking new and/or unique career opportunities. Perhaps some of the long-established fields, although they may have very favorable employment outlooks, hold little or no appeal for you. Perhaps you might even like to take your chances at employment in careers where the total number of workers is small and opportunities are limited as long as the positions are different and have a dynamic attraction for you.

This point of view was expressed by a group of young people with whom I recently had a discussion about their future careers.

"I don't want to be a secretary," said Susie.

"My father's an automobile mechanic, but that's not for me," Michael stated firmly. "I need excitement, a career that's different."

"And I don't want to become a teacher," exclaimed Jennifer. "Everyone in my family is a teacher."

Bobby interjected, "There's one field I don't want to end up in and that's accounting."

"Me too," agreed Betty. "My mother's an accountant. I want to do something different."

"My father's an accountant," said Bobby, "and so are my two uncles. That's enough accountants in one family," he added. "I'd like to find out what's new that I could become. I don't want a career where there are thousands of people doing the same things. There are so many thousands of accountants. I want a career in a field where there wouldn't be too many people doing what I'd be doing."

"Exactly. That's exactly the way I feel." This comment came from Ronnie, whose father is a dentist and whose mother is a social worker. "I'd like to do something new, something unique."

Melanie, whose father is a physician and whose mother is a nurse, said, "The field itself can be hundreds of years old. I don't mind that. Like medicine and nursing. They're thousands of years old and there are hundreds of thousands of physicians and nurses.

"But," continued Melanie, "inside medicine and nursing, there are smaller groups of specialists who have very unusual careers. My father's in nuclear medicine. He can look right into the insides of patients by means of scanners and see what doctors were never able to see before. And my mother's a nurse-midwife. She helps bring babies into the world. That's exciting. That's unique. That's what I'd like, a career that's unique."

The words "new," "different," and "unique" have been cropping up constantly in career discussions I've had with young people, and with older people too. Perhaps you too want to do something "different," something that you view as "new" and "unique."

All right then, let's consider some careers that are new and unique.

2

The Boom in Atomic Energy

When they hear the words "atomic energy," most people immediately think of the atomic bomb and atomic explosions. However, there is so very much more to atomic energy than an explosive "boom." There is far more that is positive than is negative in this field, and it is the new career opportunities in the field of atomic energy that are truly "booming."

The atomic energy field is quite young. It is less than forty years since the harnessing of the atom. Since the explosions of the first bomb, the emphasis has shifted from military to peaceful applications of atomic energy.

The use of atomic energy for peaceful purposes has been growing ever so rapidly in recent years. This has given rise to many new careers. During 1977, approximately three-hundred thousand people were employed in the many different aspects of the burgeoning field of atomic energy. The majority of these people were employed in the following segments of this industry: design and engineering of nuclear facilities, reactor-component design and manufacturing, research and development in

14

atomic energy, and weapons development and production. There is a large concentration of scientists, engineers, and technicians in the atomic-energy field.

Atomic-energy (nuclear) research scientists are busily at work discovering more and more about the potentials of atomic energy for peaceful purposes. Today, atomic energy is serving as a source of heat and radiation that have peaceful as well as military uses. As the years go on, scientists will find new and more efficient means of using this energy for the improvement of our well-being.

When an atomic bomb is detonated, atomic energy is released. For peaceful, commercial purposes, the release of this energy is controlled. Nuclear reactors have come about as a result of this controlled fission. The commercial electricity generated by the steam produced by nuclear reactors is one of the very important products of atomic energy. These reactors generate power for a vast variety of industrial, commercial, and other uses to help us in our daily activities.

In addition to the scientists, there are the *atomic-energy (nuclear) engineers* and *technicians* who are employed—and playing essential roles—in research and development in this field. The specific atomic-energy research and development work performed by these engineers and technicians varies with their place of employment, such as government agencies, industrial and manufacturing concerns, nuclear facilities, power plants, research laboratories, and universities. Some are involved in basic and applied nuclear research and development; others design nuclear instruments, nuclear reactors, and other equipment; and yet others test miscellaneous equipment and materials.

These engineers should be trained in the new specialty of nuclear engineering. However, since this specialty is so young, many engineers who received their training in other branches of engineering, such as chemical, civil, electrical, mechanical, and metallurgical, are employed in the atomic-energy field. Similarly, the technicians should be trained in nuclear technology. As we go through the 1980s, this specialized training will be required for entry into the scientific and technical careers in this field.

Nuclear engineers plan and conduct nuclear research to discover, test, prove, or modify nuclear theories pertaining to the release, control, and use of nuclear energy. They monitor nuclear tests and examine the operations of facilities which process or use radioactive or fissionable materials; they do this to insure efficient functioning and conformity with safety laws, regulations, and specifications. They evaluate findings in order to develop new concepts of thermonuclear analysis and new uses of radioactive processes.

Hot-cell technicians set up and operate remote-controlled equipment to test radioactive materials that are in " hot cells." These cells are special rooms enclosed with radiation shielding materials, such as concrete and lead. From outside these cells, they control what are known as "slave manipulators"; these are mechanical devices that serve as a pair of arms and hands. By means of these manipulators, technicians are able to perform chemical and metallurgical tests with radioactive materials. They may also enter the hot cells to decontaminate the cells and the equipment and to set up technical experiments; they don protective clothing before they enter the cells.

There are also special *decontamination workers* who decontaminate radioactive equipment and materials.

They utilize special radiation-detection instruments to find any and all materials that have been exposed to radiation.

Nuclear-reactor operators work in nuclear power stations, where they control the operation of nuclear reactors. They do this to create fissionable materials used for research purposes, to study the structure of atoms, and to determine the properties of materials. They activate the reactor and insert objects to be irradiated. They follow the directions of the nuclear experimenters and monitor the instruments at the console and reactor panels in order to control chain reactions. They may work as members of a team and alternate between operating the reactor controls and monitoring the instruments, gages, and other recording devices in the control room. Approximately two thousand persons were employed as reactor operators in 1977.

Radiation monitors are also known as *health-physics technicians*. They use radiation detectors and other special instruments to monitor plant facilities, personnel, and work environments in order to detect radioactive contamination. They measure the intensity, and identify the type, of radiation in working areas, using devices such as beta-gamma survey meters, gamma-background monitors, and alpha-beta-gamma counters. They consider such factors as maximum radiation-exposure limits and the radiation levels and thereby determine the amount of time that employees may work in contaminated areas. They also prescribe safety precautions for those who enter radiation zones and collect and analyze radiation detectors, such as film badges and pocket detection chambers, worn by workers. In 1977, there were approximately twenty-four hundred radiation monitors working in the field of atomic energy. These technicians generally serve under the supervision of *radiation physicists.*

Radiation physicists are known, too, as *health physicists* or *radiological physicists.* This is a very young occupation, and there are probably no more than one thousand of these physicists at present working on radiation protection and research or the teaching of this subject. They are involved in the detection of radiation and the application of safety standards to control exposure to radiation. They devise and manage research, training, and monitoring programs to protect plant and laboratory personnel from radiation hazards. They plan and organize radiological health programs at atomic-energy plants. They advise on methods of dealing with radiation hazards and perform research studies on the effects of human exposure to radiation.

Radiographers are also known as *industrial X-ray operators.* They take radiographs of metal castings, weldments, metal samples, and other objects to detect flaws, cracks, and the presence of foreign objects. They do this by adjusting the controls of an X-ray machine, or by exposing to a source of radioactivity the object that is to be radiographed. They use radiation meters to verify radiation intensities.

The use of radioisotopes is another essential application of atomic energy. *Radioisotope-production operators* control varied laboratory equipment to prepare radioisotopes and other radioactive materials that are used as tracers for biological, biomedical, physiological, and industrial purposes. They place specified amounts of chemicals into container to be irradiated at the nuclear reactor or with other irradiation equipment. They perform miscellaneous chemical analyses to make certain that the radioisotopes conform to strict specifications and then prepare these radioisotopes for shipment.

It is anticipated that employment opportunities in the field of atomic energy will expand rapidly throughout the 1980s. The field is expected to grow particularly in research and development expenditures. This growth will also necessitate increases in uranium mining and milling and the production of special materials for reactors. Approximately 50 percent of all workers in the atomic-energy field are employed by the government. Most of the remainder are found in industrial organizations, nonprofit institutions, and college and university laboratories.

If the world of atomic energy is of interest to you, you should consider obtaining the appropriate preparation. Preparation for entry into the aforementioned careers involves training in nuclear engineering, nuclear physics, and the nuclear technologies.

Following are the names and addresses of institutions of higher education that offer four- and more year programs in *nuclear engineering* leading to bachelor's, master's, and doctor's degrees, with the B, M, and D indicating the specific degree program(s) offered.

Bethel College, Mishawaka, Ind. 46544 (B)

Brigham Young University, Provo, Utah 84602 (B, M)

Brown University, Providence, R.I. 02912 (B, M, D)

California State University at Northridge, Northridge, Calif. 91330 (B)

Carnegie-Mellon University, Pittsburgh, Pa. 15213 (M, D)

Catholic University of America, Washington, D.C. 20064 (B, M)

Clarkson College of Technology, Potsdam, N.Y. 13676 (B)

Columbia University School of Engineering and Applied Science, New York, N.Y. 10027 (B, M, D)

Georgia Institute of Technology, Atlanta, Ga. 30332 (B, M, D)

Howard University, Washington, D.C. 20059 (B)

Idaho State University, Pocatello, Idaho 83209 (M)

Indiana Institute of Technology, Fort Wayne, Ind. 46803 (B)

Iowa State University of Science and Technology, Ames, Iowa 50011 (M, D)

Kansas State University, Manhattan, Kans. 66506 (B, M, D)

Louisiana State University and Agricultural & Mechanical College, Baton Rouge, La. 70803 (M)

Manhattan College, Bronx, N.Y. 10471 (B)

Massachusetts Institute of Technology, Cambridge, Mass. 02139 (B, M, D)

Mississippi State University, State College, Miss. 39762 (B, M)

Mount Marty College, Yankton, S. Dak. 57078 (B)

North Carolina State University, Raleigh, N.C. 27607 (B, M, D)

Northwestern University, Evanston, Ill. 60201 (B, M, D)

Ohio State University, Columbus, Ohio 43210 (M, D)

Oregon State University, Corvallis, Oreg. 97331 (B, M, D)

Pennsylvania State University, University Park, Pa. 16802 (B, M, D)
Polytechnic Institute of New York, Brooklyn, N.Y. 11201 (B, M, D)
Princeton University, Princeton, N.J. 08540 (D)
Purdue University, West Lafayette, Ind. 47907 (B, M, D)
Rensselaer Polytechnic Institute, Troy, N.Y. 12181 (B, M, D)
State University of New York, Buffalo, N.Y. 14214 (B, M, D)
State University of New York Maritime College, Fort Schuyler, Bronx, N.Y. 10465 (B)
Texas A & M University, College Station, Tex. 77843 (B, M, D)
Tuskegee Institute, Tuskegee Institute, Ala. 36088 (M)
University of Arizona, Tucson, Ariz. 85721 (B, M, D)
University of California at Berkeley, Berkeley, Calif. 94720 (B, M, D)
University of California at Santa Barbara, Santa Barbara, Calif. 93106 (B, M)
University of Cincinnati, Cincinnati, Ohio 45221 (B, M, D)
University of Florida, Gainesville, Fla. 32611 (B, M, D)
University of Idaho, Moscow, Idaho 83843 (M)
University of Illinois at Urbana-Champaign, Urbana, Ill. 61801 (M, D)
University of Kentucky, Lexington, Ky. 40506 (M)
University of Lowell, Lowell, Mass. 01854 (B, M)

University of Maryland, College Park, Md. 20742 (M, D)

University of Michigan, Ann Arbor, Mich. 48109 (B, M, D)

University of Missouri, Columbia, Mo. 65201 (M, D)

University of Missouri, Rolla, Mo. 65401 (B, M, D)

University of New Mexico, Albuquerque, N. Mex. 87131 (M, D)

University of Oklahoma, Norman, Okla. 73109 (B, M, D)

University of Pennsylvania, Philadelphia, Pa. 19104 (M, D)

University of Rhode Island, Kingston, R.I. 02881 (M)

University of Tennessee, Knoxville, Tenn. 37916 (B, M)

University of Toledo, Toledo, Ohio 43606 (M)

University of Utah, Salt Lake City, Utah 84112 (B, M, D)

University of Virginia, Charlottesville, Va. 22903 (B, M, D)

University of Washington, Seattle, Wash. 98105 (M, D)

University of Wisconsin-Madison, Madison, Wis. 53706 (B, M, D)

Virginia Polytechnic Institute and State University, Blacksburg, Va. 24061 (M)

Worcester Polytechnic Institute, Worcester, Mass. 01609 (B, M)

Following are the names and addresses of institutions of higher education that offer four- and more year programs in *nuclear physics* leading to bachelor's, master's, and doctor's degrees, with the B, M, and D indicating the specific degree program(s) offered:

Baylor University, Waco, Tex. 76706 (B)
Brigham Young University, Provo, Utah 84602 (B, M, D)
Brown University, Providence, R.I. 02912 (B, M, D)
Carnegie-Mellon University, Pittsburgh, Pa. 15213 (M, D)
Case Western Reserve University, Cleveland, Ohio 44106 (D)
Dordt College, Sioux Center, Iowa 51250 (B)
Drexel University, Philadelphia, Pa. 19104 (M, D)
Howard University, Washington, D.C. 20059 (M, D)
Iowa State University of Science and Technology, Ames, Iowa 50011 (D)
Johns Hopkins University, Baltimore, Md. 21218 (B, D)
Kansas State University, Manhattan, Kans. 66506 (B, M)
Marlboro College, Marlboro, Vt. 05344 (B)
Massachusetts Institute of Technology, Cambridge, Mass. 02139 (B, M, D)
McGill University, Montreal, Quebec, Canada (B, M, D)
Nebraska Wesleyan University, Lincoln, Nebr. 68504 (B)
Northwestern University, Evanston, Ill. 60201 (B, M, D)

Ohio State University, Columbus, Ohio 43210 (B, M, D)
Ohio University, Athens, Ohio 45701 (M, D)
Princeton University, Princeton, N.J. 08540 (D)
Purdue University, West Lafayette, Ind. 47907 (M, D)
University of California at Berkeley, Berkeley, Calif. 94720 (B, M, D)
University of Chicago, Chicago, Ill. 60637 (M, D)
University of Denver, Denver, Colo. 80208 (B)
University of Maryland, College Park, Md. 20742 (M, D)
University of Montana, Missoula, Mont. 59812 (B, M)
University of Pennsylvania, Philadelphia, Pa. 19104 (M, D)
University of Rochester, Rochester, N.Y. 14627 (M, D)
University of Texas at Austin, Austin, Tex. 78712 (M, D)
University of Wisconsin-Eau Claire, Eau Claire, Wis. 54701 (B)
Valparaiso University, Valparaiso, Ind. 46383 (B)
Washington University, St. Louis, Mo. 63130 (B, M, D)
West Virginia Wesleyan College, Buckhannon, W. Va. 26201 (B)
Worcester Polytechnic Institute, Worcester, Mass. 01609 (B)

Following are the names and addresses of institutions of higher education that offer two-year major programs in *nuclear technology* leading to the associate degree:

Central Virginia Community College, Lynchburg,
   Va. 24502
Chattanooga State Technical Community College,
   Chattanooga, Tenn. 37406
Community College of Allegheny County, West
   Mifflin, Pa. 15122
Community College of Beaver County, Monaca, Pa.
   15061
Hartford State Technical College, Hartford, Conn.
   06106
Pennsylvania State University, University Park, Pa.
   16802
Roane State Community College, Harrington, Tenn.
   37748
Southern Technical Institute, Marietta, Ga. 30060
Terra Technical College, Fremont, Ohio 43420
Texas State Technical Institute: Waco, Tex. 76705
Texas State Technical Institute: Rio Grande, Harlin-
   gen, Tex. 78550
Trident Technical College, Charleston, S.C. 29411
Xavier University, Cincinnati, Ohio 45207

If you would like further information about careers,
research programs, and safety requirements in the field of
atomic energy, write to: U.S. Energy Research and Development Administration, Washington, D.C. 20545;
and U.S. Nuclear Regulatory Commission, Washington,
D.C. 20555.

3
Nuclear–Uniquier–Medicine

Harnessing of the atom has had many vital reverberations in the field of medicine. Of greatest importance has been the birth of a new medical specialty known as *nuclear medicine*. The specialist in this branch of medicine is called a *nuclear-medicine physician*. There are as yet few medical doctors who are referred to by this title, since this specialty is so very new.

Most of today's nuclear-medicine physicians are *radiologists* with a number of years of experience in the specialty of radiology. *Radiologists* are medical doctors who specialize in the diagnosis and treatment of diseases of the human body by means of X-rays and radioactive substances; they may specialize in diagnostic radiology (*diagnostic radiologist*) or radiation therapy (*radiation therapist*). They may diagnose and treat diseases by means of radioisotopes and be known as a *nuclear-medicine physician* or *doctor of nuclear medicine*.

William Roentgen discovered X-rays in 1895. More than half a century passed before significant improvements and advances were made in this valuable tool for disease detection. It was not until 1961 that the "scanner" known as CAT (computerized axial tomography) was invented and it did not come into popular use until the 1970s. At first, this scanner was greeted with skepticism, for it was extremely expensive and there was doubt that it could provide the radiologists with the additional information they were seeking about the malfunctioning of their patients' insides. Tremendous refinements of scanners have taken place and these machines are now invaluable in helping radiologists arrive at very delicate diagnoses.

Scanners have truly created a revolution in radiology. By the mid-1970s, all large hospitals and departments of radiology and nuclear medicine clamored for scanners. The CAT body scanner enables radiologists to view areas of their patients' bodies hitherto hidden from their view. As the patient is moved through this machine, a rotating X-ray beam picks up information from the patient's body and conveys it to a computer which interprets it. This produces a cross-sectional image, a picture, that resembles a horizontal slice of the patient's body.

Scanners can produce brain scans, bone scans, liver scans, and scans of other organs and areas of the body, which provide the nuclear-medicine physicians with remarkable images that aid them in diagnosing diseased areas of the body. These scanners are especially important in the location and identification of tumors and lesions. The information they yield is of special importance in the treatment of cancer. The scanning process often makes exploratory surgery unnecessary and reduces the number of days a patient must stay in the hospital.

A radioactive substance (also known as a radiopharmaceutical), specific for the organ being examined, is injected into the bloodstream of the patient who is to undergo scanning. *Nuclear-medicine specialists,* including the physicians, *nuclear-medicine chemists, nuclear-medicine physicists,* and *nuclear-medicine technicians,* are involved in the preparation and administration of many and varied radiopharmaceutical materials employed in scanning, diagnosis, treatment, and the monitoring of therapy.

After this radiopharmaceutical has passed through the patient's body to the specific organ under examination, the patient lies down on a special table. A gamma camera overhead then slowly "scans" the patient's body, detecting the distribution and amount of radiation in the area being examined. An image is then recorded on tape and it simultaneously appears on a televisionlike screen. Film transparencies are made from these images and any abnormalities present are visible to the physician.

When the physician wishes to determine whether a cancer patient's malignancy has spread from one organ to another, he may request that a liver scan, for example, be conducted. Scanning, however, is used not just for cancer patients, but for patients suffering from symptoms of other illnesses too. Scanning is a painless, noninvasive procedure. The machinery and the procedures are very young; their potential for aiding physicians in the detection and diagnosis of disease is tremendous and has just begun to be tapped.

If you would like to become a *radiologist,* you must first become a physician. This means you must obtain your bachelor's degree, successfully complete four years of medical school and be awarded the doctor of medicine

(M.D.) degree. This must be followed by a hospital internship and a hospital residency training program in radiology. Additional information about the career of the diagnostic radiologist may be obtained by writing to the American College of Radiology, 20 North Wacker Drive, Chicago, Ill. 60606.

Perhaps you would like to become a *radiation therapist* (also known as a *therapeutic radiologist* or *radiation oncologist*) and treat illnesses by means of radiation. Radiation therapy is the treatment of cancer, and to a much lesser degree some other illnesses, with the use of ionizing radiation, such as cobalt. Although radiation has been used in Europe for more than half a century as one of the modes of treatment for cancer patients, it was not until the late 1950s that radiation therapy began to receive significant acceptance as a mode of cancer treatment in the United States.

To become a radiation therapist, the medical-school graduate must complete a four-year residency in radiology, which includes specialized training in radiation therapy. Since, in this country, this is such a very young medical specialty, there are only about twelve hundred full-time radiation therapists in the United States. Most of them are members of the American College of Radiology and of the American Society of Therapeutic Radiologists. For further information about this specialty, write to the American Society of Therapeutic Radiologists, 20 North Wacker Drive, Chicago, Ill. 60606.

If you would like to become a *nuclear-medicine physician,* here, too, you must first become a medical doctor. This must be followed by a one-year hospital internship, training in internal medicine, pathology, and radiology;

and a two-year residency training program in nuclear medicine. Additional information about the nuclear-medicine physician may be obtained from the American Board of Nuclear Medicine, 475 Park Ave. South, New York, N.Y. 10016. This board was formed in 1971 and is a Conjoint Board of the American Board of Internal Medicine, the American Board of Pathology, and the American Board of Radiology, and is also sponsored by the Society of Nuclear Medicine.

If you would like further information about the medical profession, in general, and additionally about some of the careers discussed in this chapter, write to the American Medical Association, 535 North Dearborn St., Chicago, Ill. 60610.

Nuclear-medicine technologists carry out the actual scanning procedures whereby the organ-scan images are produced. They work under the supervision of the doctor of nuclear medicine who interprets these images, just as the *radiologic (X-ray) technologist* X-rays the patients and the radiologist interprets these X-rays. Nuclear-medicine technologists are also known as *radioisotope technologists*. Using a variety of radioisotope equipment, they prepare, administer, and measure radiopharmaceuticals for therapeutic, diagnostic and tracer studies. Since scanning procedures have only recently been perfected, the number of these technologists is very small.

Some nuclear-medicine technologists work with ultrasound. The diagnostic role of the harmless sonic boom is very, very new. Ultrasound equipment has just begun to appear in the nuclear-medicine departments of large hospitals. As yet, the scans produced by ultrasound have certain limitations, but the technology in this field is progressing rapidly and *ultrasonographers* (specialists in ultrasound) predict that as time goes on, ultrasound will play an increasingly important role in the physician's therapeutic and diagnostic armamentarium.

Technologists who subject patients to radiation and X-ray therapy are specifically known as *radiation-therapy technologists*. These technologists administer the prescribed treatment to the patient under the supervision of the radiation therapist. The college training programs for radiation-therapy technologists are as yet limited. There are a number of large hospitals that offer two-year training programs in radiation-therapy technology. If you would like to learn more about a career as a radiation-therapy technologist, check with the hospitals in your city to determine whether or not they have such training programs. If they do not, ask the directors of their nuclear-medicine and radiotherapy departments to recommend the colleges which offer approved training programs.

Numerous institutions of higher education offer two-year (associate) degree programs in radiologic technology. These programs may include courses in nuclear medicine and ultrasound, in addition to the courses in X-ray technology. Some of these institutions and others offer four- and more year (bachelor, master, and doctor) degree programs in the radiologic/nuclear-medicine technologies. It would be wise to write to the admissions officers and check the catalogues of the schools you might like to attend to determine whether their programs include nuclear medicine and ultrasound, if that is what you desire, in addition to radiologic technology.

Following are the names and addresses of institutions of higher education that offer two- and more year programs in the *radiologic technologies* leading to associate's, bachelor's, master's, and doctor's degrees, with the A, B, M, and D indicating the specific degree program(s) offered:

Alabama Christian College, Montgomery, Ala. 36109 (A)

Alderson-Broaddus College, Philippi, W. Va. 26416 (B)

Amarillo College, Amarillo, Tex. 79178 (A)

Angelina College, Lufkin, Tex. 75901 (A)

Arizona State University, Tempe, Ariz. 85281 (B)

Austin Community College, Austin, Tex. 78768 (A)

Avila College, Kansas City, Mo. 64145 (B)

Baptist College, Charleston, S.C. 29411 (B)

Bellevue Community College, Bellevue, Wash. 98007 (A)

Boise State University, Boise, Idaho 83725 (A)

Brevard Community College, Cocoa, Fla. 32922 (A)

Broome Community College, Binghamton, N.Y. 13902 (A)

Broward Community College, Fort Lauderdale, Fla. 33301 (A)

Brunswick Junior College, Brunswick, Ga. 31520 (A)

Bunker Hill Community College, Charlestown, Mass. 02129 (A)

Cabrillo College, Aptos, Calif. 95003 (A)

Calhoun (John C.) State Community College, Decatur, Ala. 35602 (A)

California State University, Northridge, Calif. 91330 (B)

Carey (William) College, Hattiesburg, Miss. 39401 (B)

Carteret Technical Institute, Morehead City, N.C. 28557 (A)

Central Ohio Technical College, Newark, Ohio 43055 (A)

Central Virginia Community College, Lynchburg, Va. 24502 (A)

Central YMCA Community College, Chicago, Ill. 60185 (A)

Chattanooga State Technical Community College, Chattanooga, Tenn. 37406 (A)

College Misericordia, Dallas, Pa. 18612 (A)

College of DuPage, Glen Ellyn, Ill. 60137 (A)

College of Lake County, Grayslake, Ill. 60030 (A)

College of the Mainland, Texas City, Tex. 77590 (A)

College of the Ozarks, Clarksville, Ark. 72830 (B)

Columbia State Community College, Columbia, Tenn. 38401 (A)

Community College of Denver, Denver, Colo. 80204 (A)

Concordia College, Milwaukee, Wis. 53208 (A)

Creighton University, Omaha, Nebr. 68178 (B)

Dakota Wesleyan University, Mitchell, S. Dak. 57301 (A)

De Paul University, Chicago, Ill. 60604 (B)

Duquesne University, Pittsburgh, Pa. 15219 (B)

Edison (Thomas A.) College, Princeton, N.J. 08540 (A)

El Paso Community College, El Paso, Tex. 79904
(A)
Elon College, Elon College, N.C. 27244 (B)
Emory University, Atlanta, Ga. 30322 (M)
Essex Community College, Baltimore, Md. 21237
(A)
Fairleigh Dickinson University, Florham-Madison
Campus, Madison, N.J. 07940 (A, B)
Fayetteville Technical Institute, Fayetteville, N.C.
28303 (A)
Ferris State College, Big Rapids, Mich. 49307 (A)
Florida Junior College, Jacksonville, Fla. 32205 (A)
Forsyth Technical Institute, Winston-Salem, N.C.
27103 (A)
Gadsden State Junior College, Gadsden, Ala. 35903
(A)
Gainesville Junior College, Gainesville, Ga. 30501
(A)
Grand Rapids Junior College, Grand Rapids, Mich.
49502 (A)
Greensboro College, Greensboro, N.C. 27420 (B)
Greenville Technical College, Greenville, S.C. 29606
(A)
Gwynedd-Mercy College, Gwynedd Valley, Pa.
19437 (A)
Hagerstown Junior College, Hagerstown, Md. 21740
(A)
Hannibal-La Grange College, Hannibal, Mo. 63401
(A)
Harrisburg Area Community College, Harrisburg,
Pa. 17110 (A)

Hillsborough Community College, Tampa, Fla. 33622 (A)

Hiwassee College, Madisonville, Tenn. 37354 (A)

Hood College, Frederick, Md. 21701 (B)

Houston Community College, Houston, Tex. 77007 (A)

Howard University, Washington, D.C. 20059 (A, B)

Hudson Valley Community College, Troy, N.Y. 12180 (A)

Idaho State University, Pocatello, Idaho 83209 (A, B)

Illinois Valley Community College, Oglesby, Ill. 61348 (A)

Incarnate Word College, San Antonio, Tex. 78209 (B)

Indian River Community College, Fort Pierce, Fla. 33450 (A)

Indiana State University, Evansville, Ind. 47712 (A)

Indiana University, Kokomo, Ind. 46901 (A)

Indiana University Northwest, Gary, Ind. 46408 (A)

Indiana University–Purdue University, Fort Wayne, Ind. 46805 (A)

Indiana University–Purdue University, Indianapolis, Ind. 46202 (A, B)

Indiana Vocational Technical College, Indianapolis, Ind. 46202 (A)

Jackson Community College, Jackson, Mich. 49201 (A)

Jefferson (Thomas) University College of Allied Health Sciences, Philadelphia, Pa. 19107 (B)

Jewell (William) College, Liberty, Mo. 64068 (B)

Johnston Technical Institute, Smithfield, N.C. 27577 (A)

Jones County Junior College, Ellisville, Miss. 39437 (A)

Kean College, Union, N.J. 07083 (B)

Kentucky Wesleyan College, Owensboro, Ky. 42301 (A)

La Grange College, La Grange, Ga. 30240 (A)

Lake Michigan College, Benton Harbor, Mich. 49022 (A)

Laramie County Community College, Cheyenne, Wyo. 82001 (A)

Lamar University, Beaumont, Texas 77710 (A)

Lawson State Community College, Birmingham, Ala. 35211 (A)

Lincoln Land Community College, Springfield, Ill. 62708 (A)

Livingston University, Livingston, Ala. 35470 (A)

Long Island University, Brooklyn, N.Y. 11201 (B)

Lorain County Community College, Elyria, Ohio 44035 (A)

Madisonville Community College, Madisonville, Ky. 42431 (A)

Madonna College, Livonia, Mich. 48150 (B)

Manhattan College, Bronx, N.Y. 10471 (A, B)

McLennon Community College, Waco, Tex. 76708 (A)

Medical College of Georgia, Augusta, Ga. 30901 (A, B)

Merced College, Merced, Calif. 95340 (A)

Mercer County Community College, Trenton, N.J. 08690 (A)

Miami-Dade Community College, Miami, Fla. 33132 (A)

Mid-Michigan Community College, Harrison, Mich. 48625 (A)

Middlesex Community College, Middletown, Conn. 06457 (A)

Middlesex County College, Edison, N.J. 08817 (A)

Midwestern State University, Wichita Falls, Tex. 76308 (A, B)

Millikin University, Decatur, Ill. 62522 (B)

Milwaukee Area Technical College, Milwaukee, Wis. 53203 (A)

Minot State College, Minot, N. Dak. 58701 (B)

Missouri Southern State College, Joplin, Mo. 64801 (A)

Monroe Community College, Rochester, N.Y. 14623 (A)

Montgomery College, Rockville, Md. 20850 (A)

Morehead State University, Morehead, Ky. 40351 (A)

Morris Harvey College, Charleston, W. Va. 25304 (A)

Mount Marty College, Yankton, S. Dak. 57078 (A, B)

Mount San Antonio College, Walnut, Calif. 91789 (A)

Mountain Empire Community College, Big Stone Gap, Va. 24219 (A)

Nassau Community College, Garden City, N.Y. 11530 (A)

Navarro College, Corsicana, Tex. 75110 (A)

Nebraska Wesleyan University, Lincoln, Nebr. 68504 (A)

New Hampshire Technical Institute, Concord, N.H. 03301 (A)

New Mexico State University, Las Cruces, N. Mex. 88003 (A)

North Country Community College, Saranac Lake, N.Y. 12983 (A)

North Shore Community College, Beverly, Mass. 01915 (A)

Northampton County Area Community College, Bethlehem, Pa. 18017 (A)

Northeast Louisiana University, Monroe, La. 71203 (B)

Northeastern University, Boston, Mass. 02115 (A, M)

Northern Arizona University, Flagstaff, Ariz. 86011 (B)

Northern Essex Community College, Haverhill, Mass. 01830 (A)

Northern Kentucky University, Highland Heights, Ky. 41076 (A)

Oakton Community College, Morton Grove, Ill. 60053 (A)

Odessa College, Odessa, Tex. 79760 (A)

Ohio State University, Columbus, Ohio 43210 (B)

Orange Coast College, Costa Mesa, Calif. 92626 (A)

Oregon Institute of Technology, Klamath Falls, Oreg. 97601 (A, B)

Oscar Rose Junior College, Midwest City, Okla. 73110 (A)

Otterbein College, Westerville, Ohio 43081 (A)

Ottumwa Heights College, Ottumwa, Iowa 52501 (A)

Owens (Michael J.) Technical College, Toledo, Ohio 43699 (A)

Palm Beach Junior College, Lake Worth, Fla. 33461 (A)

Paris Junior College, Paris, Tex. 75460 (A)

Parkersburg Community College, Parkersburg, W. Va. 26101 (A)

Penn Valley Community College, Kansas City, Mo. 64111 (A)

Piedmont Technical College, Greenwood, S.C. 29646 (A)

Pima Community College, Tucson, Ariz. 85709 (A)

C. W. Post College (Long Island University), Greenvale, N.Y. 11548 (B, M)

Presentation College, Aberdeen, S. Dak. 57401 (A)

Prince George's Community College, Largo, Md. 20870 (A)

Quinnipiac College, Hamden, Conn. 06518 (A, B)

Reading Area Community College, Reading, Pa. 19603 (A)

Roane State Community College, Harriman, Tenn. 37748 (A)

Rhode Island Junior College, Warwick, R.I. 02886 (A)

Robert Morris College, Coraopolis, Pa. 15108 (A)

Roosevelt University, Chicago, Ill. 60605 (B)

St. Cloud State University, St. Cloud, Minn. 56301 (B)

St. Joseph's College, North Windham, Maine 04062
(B)
St. Louis University, St. Louis, Mo. 63103 (B)
St. Philip's College, San Antonio, Tex. 78203 (A)
Salem College, Salem, W. Va. 26426 (B)
Santa Barbara City College, Santa Barbara, Calif.
93109 (A)
Santa Rosa Junior College, Santa Rosa, Calif. 95401
(A)
Scott Community College, Bettendorf, Iowa 52722
(A)
Shelby State Community College, Memphis, Tenn.
38104 (A)
Sinclair Community College, Dayton, Ohio 45402
(A)
South Plains College, Levelland, Tex. 79336 (A)
Southeast Community College, Lincoln, Nebr. 68501
(A)
Springfield Technical Community College, Spring-
field, Mass. 01105 (A)
State University of New York Downstate Medical
Center, Brooklyn, N.Y. 11203 (A)
Syracuse University, Syracuse, N.Y. 13210 (B, M,
D)
Tarrant County Junior College, Fort Worth, Tex.
76102 (A)
Texas Southmost College, Brownsville, Tex. 78520
(A)
Trident Technical College, Charleston, S.C. 29411
(A)
Triton College, River Grove, Ill. 60171 (A)
Trocaire College, Buffalo, N.Y. 14220 (A)

University of Alabama, Birmingham, Ala. 35294
(B)

University of Albuquerque, Albuquerque, N. Mex.
87140 (A, D)

University of California, Irvine, Calif. 92717 (M,
D)

University of Central Arkansas, Conway, Ark.
72032 (B)

University of Cincinnati, Cincinnati, Ohio 45221
(A)

University of Chicago, Chicago, Ill. 60637 (M)

University of Evansville, Evansville, Ind. 47702 (A)

University of Idaho, Moscow, Idaho 83843 (M)

University of Iowa, Iowa City, Iowa 52242 (B)

University of Kentucky, Lexington, Ky. 40506 (M)

University of Michigan, Ann Arbor, Mich. 48109
(B, M)

University of Minnesota, Twin Cities, Minneapolis,
Minn. 55455 (A)

University of Missouri, Columbia, Mo. 65201 (B)

University of Nevada, Las Vegas, Nev. 89154 (A,
B)

University of New Mexico, Albuquerque, N. Mex.
87131 (A)

University of North Carolina, Chapel Hill, N.C.
27514 (B)

University of Oklahoma Health Sciences Center,
Oklahoma City, Okla. 73190 (B, M, D)

University of Pittsburgh, Pittsburgh, Pa. 15260 (M)

University of Tennessee Center for the Health
Sciences, Memphis, Tenn. 38163 (B)

University of Vermont, Burlington, Vt. 05401 (A)

University of Washington, Seattle, Wash. 98105 (M)

University of Wisconsin, Madison, Wis. 53706 (M, D)

Valdosta State College, Valdosta, Ga. 31601 (A)

Virginia Commonwealth University, Richmond, Va. 23284 (A)

Virginia Western Community College, Roanoke, Va. 24015 (A)

Washtenaw Community College, Ann Arbor, Mich. 48106 (A)

Wayne State University, Detroit, Mich. 48202 (B, M)

Weber State College, Ogden, Utah 84408 (A)

Wenatchee Valley College, Wenatchee, Wash. 98801 (A)

Westchester Community College, Valhalla, N.Y. 10595 (A)

Western Kentucky University, Bowling Green, Ky. 42101 (A)

Wheeling College, Wheeling, W. Va. 26003 (B)

Widener College, Chester, Pa. 19013 (B)

Wittenberg University, Springfield, Ohio 45501 (B)

Xavier University, Cincinnati, Ohio 45207 (A)

The need for nuclear-medicine and radiation-therapy technologists is great and the demand far exceeds the supply. It is anticipated that the employment outlook for these technologists will be excellent throughout the 1980s for those who are appropriately trained and who have the interest and ability to work with sick people. They must be compassionate, considerate, and courteous to patients.

They must also possess a keen sense of responsibility, a great deal of integrity, and the ability to work with extreme accuracy.

Another newcomer who has joined the nuclear-medicine chemists and nuclear-medicine physicists in the medical field is the *biomedical engineer.*

Biomedical engineers employ the principles of engineering for the solution of medical and health-related problems. Pacemakers that regulate the beat of the heart and extend the lives of many people who have heart disorders were developed by biomedical engineers.

Biomedical engineers are involved too in the design and development of many unusual medical devices including lasers for surgery, artificial organs (for example, hearts and kidneys), and prostheses for amputees. They develop and perfect ultrasonic imaging devices to aid physicians in observing, diagnosing, and treating the disorders and diseases of their patients. Their combined biomedical and engineering training also enables them to adapt computers to medical science.

Following are the names and addresses of institutions of higher education that offer four- and more year programs in *biomedical engineering* leading to bachelor's, master's, and doctor's degrees, with the B, M, and D indicating the specific degree program(s) offered:

Boston University, Boston, Mass. 02215 (B)
Brigham Young University, Provo, Utah 84602 (B,
    M)

Brown University, Providence, R.I. 02912 (B, M, D)
Bucknell University, Lewisburg, Pa. 17837 (B)
California State University, Long Beach, Calif. 90840 (B)
California State University, Northridge, Calif. 91330 (B)
Carnegie-Mellon University, Pittsburgh, Pa. 15213 (B, M, D)
Case Western Reserve University, Cleveland, Ohio 44106 (B, M, D)
Catholic University of America, Washington, D.C. 20064 (B, M)
Clemson University, Clemson, S.C. 29631 (M, D)
Cleveland State University, Cleveland, Ohio 44115 (B)
Colorado Technical College, Colorado Springs, Colo. 80903 (B)
Columbia University School of Engineering and Applied Science, New York, N.Y. 10027 (B, M, D)
Cornell College, Mount Vernon, Iowa 52314 (B)
Drexel University, Philadelphia, Pa. 19104 (M, D)
Duke University, Durham, N.C. 27706 (B, M, D)
Fairleigh-Dickinson University, Teaneck-Hackensack Campus, Teaneck, N.J. 07666 (M)
George Washington University, Washington, D.C. 20052 (M, D)
Harvard University, Cambridge, Mass. 01778 (B)
Indiana University–Purdue University, Indianapolis, Ind. 46202 (B)
Iowa State University of Science and Technology, Ames, Iowa 50011 (M, D)

Johns Hopkins University, Baltimore, Md. 21218 (B, D)
Louisiana Tech University, Ruston, La. 71272 (B)
Manhattan College, Bronx, N.Y. 10471 (B)
Marquette University, Milwaukee, Wis. 53233 (B, M, D)
Massachusetts Institute of Technology, Cambridge, Mass. 02139 (B, D)
McGill University, Montreal, Quebec, Canada (M)
Messiah College, Grantham, Pa. 17027 (B)
Michigan Technological University, Houghton, Mich. 49931 (B)
Mississippi State University, State College, Miss. 39762 (B, M, D)
Mount Marty College, Yankton, S. Dak. 57078 (B)
New Jersey Institute of Technology, Newark, N.J. 07102 (B)
New York Institute of Technology, Old Westbury, N.Y. 11568 (B)
Northeastern University, Boston, Mass. 02115 (B)
Northwestern University, Evanston, Ill. 60201 (B, M, D)
Ohio State University, Columbus, Ohio 43210 (B)
Pennsylvania State University, University Park, Pa. 16802 (M, D)
Polytechnic Institute of New York, Brooklyn, N.Y. 11201 (M, D)
Princeton University, Princeton, N.J. 08540 (B)
Purdue University, West Lafayette, Ind. 47907 (B, M, D)
Radcliffe College, Cambridge, Mass. 01778 (B)

Rensselaer Polytechnic Institute, Troy, N.Y. 12181
(B, M, D)
Southern Methodist University, Dallas, Tex. 75275
(B)
Stanford University, Stanford, Calif. 94305 (M, D)
Swarthmore College, Swarthmore, Pa. 19081 (B)
Syracuse University, Syracuse, N.Y. 13210 (B)
Temple University, Philadelphia, Pa. 19122 (B)
Texas A and M University, College Station, Tex.
77843 (B, M, D)
Trinity College, Hartford, Conn. 06106 (M)
Tufts University, Medford, Mass. 02155 (M, D)
Tulane University, New Orleans, La. 70118 (B, M,
D)
University of Bridgeport, Bridgeport, Conn. 06602
(B)
University of California, Berkeley, Calif. 94702 (B,
M, D)
University of California, Davis, Calif. 95616 (D)
University of California, La Jolla, Calif. 92093 (B,
M, D)
University of Cincinnati, Cincinnati, Ohio 45221
(M, D)
University of Colorado, Boulder, Colo. 80309 (B)
University of Illinois at Chicago Circle, Chicago, Ill.
60680 (B, M, D)
University of Iowa, Iowa City, Iowa 52242 (B)
University of Miami, Coral Gables, Fla. 33124 (B,
M)
University of Michigan, Ann Arbor, Mich. 48109
(B, M, D)

University of Minnesota, Twin Cities, Minneapolis, Minn. 55455 (M, D)

University of Mississippi, University, Miss. 38677 (M, D)

University of New Mexico, Albuquerque, N. Mex. 87131 (B)

University of Oklahoma, Norman, Okla. 73019 (B)

University of Pennsylvania, Philadelphia, Pa. 19104 (B, M, D)

University of Pittsburgh, Pittsburgh, Pa. 15260 (M)

University of Rochester, Rochester, N.Y. 14627 (M, D)

University of Southern California, Los Angeles, Calif. 90007 (B, M, D)

University of Texas, Arlington, Tex. 76019 (M)

University of Texas, Austin, Tex. 78712 (D)

University of Toledo, Toledo, Ohio 43606 (B)

University of Utah, Salt Lake City, Utah 84112 (M, D)

University of Vermont, Burlington, Vt. 05401 (M)

University of Washington, Seattle, Wash. 98105 (B, M, D)

University of Wisconsin, Madison, Wis. 53706 (M)

University of Wyoming, Laramie, Wyo. 82071 (B, M, D)

Vanderbilt University, Nashville, Tenn. 37240 (B, M, D)

Washington University, St. Louis, Mo. 63130 (B, M, D)

Wichita State University, Wichita, Kans. 67208 (B)

Worcester Polytechnic Institute, Worcester, Mass. 01609 (B, M)

In 1977, there were approximately four thousand biomedical engineers. Although many work for government agencies, an increasing number are employed in the private sector, especially in hospitals and institutions, where they work at medical research and the development of new devices, instruments, techniques, and systems for the improvement of health care.

The demand for biomedical engineers far exceeds the supply and it is expected that this situation will prevail throughout the 1980s. Biomedical engineers who do graduate study beyond their bachelor's degree and obtain the master's and doctor's degrees will probably have excellent employment opportunities in medical research and teaching in colleges and universities.

For additional information about the career of the biomedical engineer, write to one or more of the following:

Alliance for Engineering in Medicine and Biology
3900 Wisconsin Ave. N.W., Suite 300
Washington, D.C. 20016

Biomedical Engineering Society
P.O. Box 2399
Culver City, Calif. 90230

Foundation for Medical Technology
Mount Sinai Hospital and Medical Center
Fifth Avenue and 100th Street
New York, N.Y. 10029

4

Careers—In and Out of This World

Explorer I, our first man-made satellite, was launched on January 31, 1958. Two decades later, on January 16, 1978, the National Aeronautics and Space Administration selected thirty-five new astronauts, among whom were six women, three black men, and one Japanese-American.

Four months before Explorer I was launched, the Soviet Union had launched Sputnik I, the first artificial satellite. The space race between the United States and the USSR thus began in earnest. In the period between 1958 and 1978, approximately 1,900 satellites, representing dozens of countries, were placed into orbit. Approximately 850, of which about 450 belong to the United States, are still orbiting the earth. Although the Russians had the lead at the start of the space race, America is now out front. In this same two-decade period, seventy-one Americans, all white males, went into space and twelve Americans walked on the moon.

The competition for joining the *astronauts* corps is extremely keen. Those who were selected to become astronauts in January 1978 constituted the first group chosen since 1969; a total of seventy-three astronauts had been selected since 1959 and twenty-seven of them were still available for space flights in 1978. More than eight thousand persons applied for the thirty-five 1978 openings. The six women who were chosen to become astronauts included a biochemist, an electrical engineer, a geologist, a physician, a physicist, and a surgeon. The training program for the group of new astronauts started in July 1978 at the Lyndon B. Johnson Space Center in Houston, Texas.

The space age that lies ahead will involve not only astronauts but *aerospace scientists, aerospace engineers, aerospace technologists and technicians,* and a vast variety of aerospace workers.

The aerospace industry is made up of companies that manufacture and assemble aircraft, missiles, and spacecraft. Piston, jet, or rocket engines may be the power that enables aircraft to function. Missiles, in turn, may be powered by either jet or rocket engines. Spacecraft are powered by rocket engines only. In contrast to aircraft, which fly within the earth's atmosphere, missiles and spacecraft travel into space. Aircraft fly at much slower speeds than missiles or spacecraft which travel many times faster than sound.

Aircraft range from small personal planes to multimillion-dollar transports and supersonic fighters. Missiles are essentially for military use. Spacecraft are used for outer space exploration or to monitor conditions within the earth's atmosphere; some enter into earth orbit and become artificial satellites.

There were approximately eight-hundred thousand persons employed in the aerospace industry in 1977. Additionally, thousands more worked for the United States government in aerospace-related activities. This industry requires the services of many different types of workers. There are three major career categories in aerospace manufacturing. They are: (1) professional and technical, (2) administrative, clerical, and related occupations, and (3) plant occupations. It is in the first category that we find the new careers unique to the world of aerospace. The other two categories of workers are not new and are found in other industries too.

Aerospace technology is constantly changing and advancing. Research and development are an essential aspect of the industry. Thus, technical personnel are extremely important here. *Engineers, scientists,* and *technicians* constitute more than 25 percent of the total workers in this industry. They work together in the development of designs for aircraft, missiles, and spacecraft. Varied engineers and scientists are involved in these and other projects. They work on a wide range of applied problems in space science.

The *aerospace engineers* and *scientists* are the new and major workers. These engineers play essential roles in our space and defense programs. They are involved in the design and development of a variety of aircraft structures, conventional aircraft, guided missiles, propulsion systems, rockets, spacecraft, and supersonic transports. Some aerospace engineers specialize in one specific type of aerospace vehicle, such as landing modules, launch vehicles, manned space capsules, or satellites.

The minimum requirement for beginner engineer or scientist positions in the aerospace industry is the baccalaureate degree in engineering or in one of the sciences. Advancement, generally, calls for graduate study leading to the master's or doctor's degrees.

Following are the names and addresses of institutions of higher education that offer four- and more year degree programs in *aerospace and astronautical engineering* leading to bachelor's, master's, and doctor's degrees, with the B, M, and D indicating the specific degree program(s) offered:

Aero-Space Institute, Chicago, Ill. 60611 (B)
Albright College, Reading, Pa. 19604 (B)
Arizona State University, Tempe, Ariz. 85281 (B, M)
Auburn University, Auburn, Ala. 36830 (B, M, D)
Baptist College, Charleston, S.C. 29411 (B)
Bethel College, Mishawaka, Ind. 46544 (B)
Boston University, Boston, Mass. 02215 (B)
Brigham Young University, Provo, Utah 84602 (B, M)
California Institute of Technology, Pasadena, Calif. 91125 (M, D)
California Polytechnic State University, San Luis Obispo, Calif. 93407 (B)
California State Polytechnic University, Pomona, Calif. 91768 (B)
California State University, Northridge, Calif. 91330 (B)
Catholic University of America, Washington, D.C. 20064 (B, M)
Cornell University, Ithaca, N.Y. 14853 (M)

Drexel University, Philadelphia, Pa. 19104 (M, D)

Embry-Riddle Aeronautical University, Daytona Beach, Fla. 32014 (B, M)

Georgia College, Milledgeville, Ga. 31061 (B)

Georgia Institute of Technology, Atlanta, Ga. 30332 (B, M, D)

Harvard College, Cambridge, Mass. 01778 (B)

Henderson State University, Arkadelphia, Ark. 71923 (B)

Hofstra University, Hempstead, N.Y. 11550 (B)

Indiana Institute of Technology, Fort Wayne, Ind. 46803 (B)

Iowa State University of Science and Technology, Ames, Iowa 50011 (B, M, D)

Kent State University, Kent, Ohio 44242 (B)

Louisiana State University & Agricultural and Mechanical College, Baton Rouge, La. 70803 (B)

Massachusetts Institute of Technology, Cambridge, Mass. 02139 (B, M, D)

McGill University, Montreal, Quebec, Canada (M)

Mississippi State University, Mississippi State, Miss. 39762 (B, M)

Mount Marty College, Yankton, S. Dak. 57078 (B)

New York Institute of Technology, Old Westbury, N.Y. 11568 (B)

North Carolina State University, Raleigh, N.C. 27607 (B)

Northrop University, Inglewood, Calif. 90306 (B, M)

Northwestern University, Evanston, Ill. 60201 (M, D)

Ohio State University, Columbus, Ohio 43210 (B, M, D)

Parks College (St. Louis University), Cahokia, Ill. 62206 (B)

Pennsylvania State University, University Park, Pa. 16802 (B, M, D)

Polytechnic Institute of New York, Brooklyn, N.Y. 11201 (B, M, D)

Princeton University, Princeton, N.J. 08540 (B, M, D)

Purdue University, West Lafayette, Ind. 47907 (B, M, D)

Radcliffe College, Cambridge, Mass. 01778 (B)

Rensselaer Polytechnic Institute, Troy, N.Y. 12181 (B, M, D)

Rice University, Houston, Tex. 77001 (M, D)

St. Louis University, St. Louis, Mo. 63103 (B)

San Diego State University, San Diego, Calif. 92182 (B, M)

San Jose State University, San Jose, Calif. 95192 (B)

Southeastern Oklahoma State University, Durant, Okla. 74701 (B)

Southern Methodist University, Dallas, Tex. 75275 (B)

Stanford University, Stanford, Calif. 94305 (M, D)

State University of New York, Buffalo, N.Y. 14214 (B, M, D)

Syracuse University, Syracuse, N.Y. 13210 (B, M, D)

Texas A & M University, College Station, Tex. 77843 (B, M, D)

Tri-State University, Angola, Ind. 46703 (B)
University of Alabama, University, Ala. 35486 (B, M)
University of Arizona, Tucson, Ariz. 85721 (B, M, D)
University of California, Berkeley, Calif. 94720 (B)
University of California, Davis, Calif. 95616 (B)
University of California at San Diego, La Jolla, Calif. 92093 (D)
University of Cincinnati, Cincinnati, Ohio 45221 (B M, D)
University of Colorado, Boulder, Colo. 80309 (B, M, D)
University of Dayton, Dayton, Ohio 45469 (M, D)
University of Delaware, Newark, Del. 19711 (M, D)
University of Florida, Gainesville, Fla. 32611 (B, M, D)
University of Illinois at Chicago Circle, Chicago, Ill. 60680 (B, M, D)
University of Illinois at Urbana-Champaign, Urbana, Ill. 61801 (B, M, D)
University of Maryland, College Park, Md. 20742 (B, M)
University of Massachusetts, Amherst, Mass. 01003 (B)
University of Michigan, Ann Arbor, Mich. 48109 (B, M, D)
University of Minnesota, Morris, Minn. 56267 (B)
University of Minnesota, Twin Cities, Minneapolis, Minn. 55455 (B, M)
University of Missouri, Columbia, Mo. 65201 (B)

University of Missouri, Rolla, Mo. 65401 (B, M, D)
University of Notre Dame, Notre Dame, Ind. 46556 (B, M, D)
University of Oklahoma, Norman, Okla. 73019 (B, M, D)
University of Pittsburgh, Pittsburgh, Pa. 15260 (B)
University of Southern California, Los Angeles, Calif. 90007 (B, M, D)
University of Tennessee, Knoxville, Tenn. 37916 (B, M, D)
University of Texas, Arlington, Tex. 76019 (B, M)
University of Texas, Austin, Tex. 78712 (B, M, D)
University of Utah, Salt Lake City, Utah 84112 (B, M)
University of Virginia, Charlottesville, Va. 22903 (B, M, D)
University of Washington, Seattle, Wash. 98105 (B, M, D)
Virginia Polytechnic Institute & State University, Blacksburg, Va. 24061 (B, M, D)
Washington University, St. Louis, Mo. 63130 (B, M, D)
West Virginia University, Morganstown, W. Va. 26505 (B, M)
Western Michigan University, Kalamazoo, Mich. 49008 (B)
Wichita State University, Wichita, Kans. 67208 (B, M)

Aeronautical and aerospace technicians assist the aerospace engineers and scientists. They participate in activities involved in varied aspects of the design and production of aircraft, guided missiles, rockets, and spacecraft. For those who have mechanical aptitude and manual dexterity and are interested in aeronautics and aerospace, but who have no desire to spend four or more years in college to get an engineering degree, there may be plentiful career opportunities as technicians if they successfully complete the two-year associate degree program in this field.

Following are the names and addresses of institutions of higher education that offer two-year programs leading to the associate degree in *aeronautical and aerospace technologies:*

Academy of Aeronautics, Flushing, N.Y. 11371
Aero-Space Institute, Chicago, Ill. 60611
Alpena Community College, Alpena, Mich. 49707
Andrews University, Berrien Springs, Mich. 49104
Asnuntuck Community College, Enfield, Conn. 06082
Broward Community College, Fort Lauderdale, Fla. 33301
Central Missouri State University, Warrensburg, Mo. 64093
Central Texas College, Killeen, Tex. 76541
Cerro Coso Community College, Ridgecrest, Calif. 93555
Cochise College, Douglas, Ariz. 85607
College of Alameda, Alameda, Calif. 94501
College of the Redwoods, Eureka, Calif. 95501
Columbus Technical Institute, Columbus, Ohio 43216
Cooke County College, Gainesville, Tex. 76240

Cuyahoga Community College, Cleveland, Ohio 44115

El Paso Community College, Colorado Springs, Colo. 80904

El Reno Junior College, El Reno, Okla. 73036

Embry-Riddle Aeronautical University, Daytona Beach, Fla. 32014

Everett Community College, Everett, Wash. 98201

Gateway Technical Institute, Kenosha, Wis. 53140

Gulf Coast Community College, Panama City, Fla. 32401

Idaho State University, Pocatello, Idaho 83209

Iowa Western Community College, Council Bluffs, Iowa 51501

Kansas Technical Institute, Salina, Kans. 67401

Kirtland Community College, Roscommon, Mich. 48653

Lane Community College, Eugene, Oreg. 97405

Lewis University, Lockport, Ill. 60441

Lorain County Community College, Elyria, Ohio 44035

Macomb County Community College, Mount Clemens, Mich. 48043

Merced College, Merced, Calif. 95340

Mercer County Community College, Trenton, N.J. 08690

Metropolitan State College, Denver, Colo. 80204

Miami-Dade Community College, Miami, Fla. 33167

Mira Costa College, Oceanside, Calif. 92054

Motlow State Community College, Tullahoma, Tenn. 37388

Mount Hood Community College, Gresham, Oreg. 97030

Mount San Antonio College, Walnut, Calif. 91789

Nicholls State University, Thibodaux, La. 70301

North Shore Community College, Beverly, Mass. 01915

Northeast Louisiana University, Monroe, La. 71203

Northeastern Oklahoma Agricultural & Mechanical College, Miami, Okla. 74354

Northeastern University, Boston, Mass. 02115

Northern Michigan University, Marquette, Mich. 49855

Northwestern Michigan College, Traverse City, Mich. 49684

Northrop University, Inglewood, Calif. 90306

Ohio University, Athens, Ohio 45701

Orange Coast College, Costa Mesa, Calif. 92626

Oscar Rose Junior College, Midwest City, Okla. 73110

Palm Beach Junior College, Lake Worth, Fla. 33461

Parks College (St. Louis University), Cahokia, Ill. 62206

Pennsylvania State University, University Park, Pa. 16802

Pima Community College, Tucson, Ariz. 85709

Purdue University, West Lafayette, Ind. 47907

St. Louis Community College at Meramec, Kirkwood, Mo. 63122

St. Petersburg Junior College, St. Petersburg, Fla. 33733

Southeastern Oklahoma State University, Durant, Okla. 74701

Southern Illinois University, Carbondale, Ill. 62901
Southwest Technical Institute, Camden, Ark. 71701
Southwestern Michigan College, Dowagiac, Mich. 49047
Spokane Community College, Spokane, Wash. 99207
State University of New York Agricultural and Technical College, Farmingdale, N.Y. 11735
Tarrant County Junior College, Fort Worth, Tex. 76102
Texarkana Community College, Texarkana, Tex. 75501
Texas State Technical Institute, Waco, Tex. 76705
Trident Technical College, Charleston, S.C. 29411
University of Alaska, Anchorage, Alaska 99504
University of Hawaii (Honolulu Community College), Honolulu, Hawaii 96817
Vincennes University, Vincennes, Ind. 47591
Wayne Community College, Goldsboro, N.C. 27350
Western Kentucky University, Bowling Green, Ky. 42101
Winona State University, Winona, Minn. 55987

The employment outlook for aerospace engineers and technicians and for the vast variety of other workers in this field appears to be good. It is anticipated that employment opportunities in the 1980s will be better than they were in the 1970s. How much better it will be will depend to a great extent on the expenditures of the federal government, inasmuch as many of the aerospace vehicles are either military hardware or space vehicles. Another determinant of employment opportunities in this field is civilian aircraft production; it is anticipated that this will remain rather stable throughout the 1980s.

Via satellites and space probes, we shall be able to obtain information hitherto unavailable. Satellites have revolutionized communications and have enabled millions of people to observe, via television, something happening thousands of miles away. Space shuttles will similarly revolutionize space travel. The peaceful potential, in such matters as moon bases, planetary exploration, and space colonies, is tremendous, and only time will tell what the space missions will yield. The future prospects are dynamic and exciting.

If you would like to obtain further information about career opportunities in aerospace, write to one or more of the following:

American Institute of Aeronautics and Astronautics
1290 Avenue of the Americas
New York, N.Y. 10019

International Union, United Automobile, Aerospace,
    and Agricultural Implement Workers of America
8000 East Jefferson Ave.
Detroit, Mich. 48214

National Aeronautics and Space Administration
Washington, D.C. 20546

5

Computing the Career Opportunities in the Computer Industry

The word "computer" became popular in our general vocabulary during the 1950s. The computer's potentials for practical applications were many and, as a result, the computer industry grew rapidly. It has since become one of our fastest growing industries.

The federal government purchased its first electronic computer in 1951 for approximately 1.5 million dollars. It was used by the U.S. Census Bureau for civilian purposes. In 1978, the United States government spent more than twelve billion dollars for computers used for civilian and military purposes.

Computers today are a very important part of our everyday life. Computer systems collect, store, and sort tremendous amounts of information. This information is called "data." Every avenue of the business and commercial world, in addition to the worlds of scientific, medical, and engineering research, relies on computer systems to solve their complex problems.

If we were to total all of the *computer-operating personnel, programmers,* and *systems analysts,* the sum would equal about 1,000,000 persons employed in this industry in 1977. More than half a million were *computer-operating personnel* of various sorts; more than a quarter of a million were computer *programmers,* and the remainder were *systems analysts.*

Keypunch operators, data typists, card-to-tape converter operators, console operators, and *tape librarians* are among the varied computer-operating personnel. *Keypunch operators* punch varied patterns of holes into cards. These holes represent different numbers, letters, and other information. The information that is processed and the instructions for the computer are termed "input"; the results are "output." Thus, the keypunch operators prepare input.

Data typists use special machines to convert the data they type to holes in cards or onto tapes or discs. Some data typists deliver the input material directly into a computer.

There are varied computer systems. Some employ only input from magnetic tapes. There are *card-to-tape converter operators* who transfer information from punched cards or paper tapes to magnetic tapes. They connect circuits by wiring plugboards according to prepared diagrams and then load the machines with cards and tapes.

Console operators are also called *computer operators.* After the input has been coded and put into a form that can be read by the computer, it is ready for processing. Here the work of the console operators begins. They examine the instructions given to them by the programmers and prepare the machinery for the "run." They see to it that the computer has been properly loaded with the correct cards, discs, or tapes. They adjust the appropriate dials and switches and then put the computer in operation. They watch the computer while it is running to be sure that everything is functioning as it should. If anything goes wrong, they must locate the problem and correct it.

Often, it is important to keep the cards, tapes, and computer programs for future use. *Tape librarians* are in charge of this task. They classify, catalog, and maintain files of punched cards, magnetic tapes, computer programs, and computer operating instructions.

The majority of computer-operating personnel are women. Many have received their training in high schools, public and private vocational schools, and business schools; others entered beginners' jobs in this field via on-the-job training. There are a great many two-year colleges that offer associate degree training programs in computer-operating occupations. The successful completion of such training programs is important if you wish to advance in this field. Check with the admissions office of your local community or junior college to determine the nature of their degree programs in computer technologies and their requirements for admission to these programs.

Among their many essential functions, computers solve very involved scientific and technical problems. However, they are machines and, therefore, cannot "think" for themselves. They can perform their functions only because *computer programmers* feed them with step-by-step instructions. By following these instructions, the computers are able to process a great deal of data accurately and rapidly. These programmers analyze the information that is to be processed or the problems that are to be solved; they then prepare step-by-step instructions for the console operators. These detailed instructions are known as "programs."

There are a multitude of different programs. They vary according to the nature of the problems to be solved. Programs designed, for example, to monitor factory production processes or to bill department-store customers or to record airplane reservations or to trace the flight path of a space probe or to determine hospital patients' reactions to a specific drug are, of necessity, quite different. Some programs are rather simple and take just a few days to prepare. Others are very complex and employ intricate mathematical and scientific formulas; they may require many months, perhaps even more than a year, of preparation time.

Only about 25 percent of the computer programmers are women. There are no specific educational requirements for programmers. Many have had one or two years of college training including courses in computer science. Some are college graduates. As time goes on, through the 1980s, the college degree will be a necessity for appointment to most programmers' positions. The completion of college courses in the physical sciences, engineering, and mathematics, as well as computer science, are required of programmers who wish to work for organizations and institutions using computers for scientific or engineering applications. Graduate degrees may be required where the work is highly scientific and complex.

Following are the names and addresses of institutions of higher education that offer associate's, bachelor's and master's degree programs in *computer programming,* with the A, B, and M indicating the specific degree program(s) offered:

Alabama Agricultural and Mechanical University, Normal, Ala. 35762 (B)

Albany Junior College, Albany, Ga. 31707 (A)

Allegany Community College, Cumberland, Md. 21502 (A)

American University, Washington, D.C. 20016 (A)

Baruch (Bernard M.) College, City University of New York, New York, N.Y. 10010 (B, M)

Baylor University, Waco, Tex. 76706 (B, M)

Berkshire Community College, Pittsfield, Mass. 01201 (A)

Black Hills State College, Spearfish, S. Dak. 57783 (A)

Bowling Green State University, Huron, Ohio 44839 (A)

Bradley University, Peoria, Ill. 61625 (B)

Brigham Young University, Provo, Utah 84602 (B, M)

Brunswick Junior College, Brunswick, Ga. 31520 (A)

Bryant College, Smithfield, R.I. 02917 (B)

Bucks County Community College, Newtown, Pa. 18940 (A)

Butler County Community College, Butler, Pa. 16001 (A)

Butler University, Indianapolis, Ind. 46208 (B)

California State College, California, Pa. 15419 (B)

Californa State University, Fresno, Calif. 93740 (B)

California State University, Fullerton, Calif. 92634
(B, M)
Calumet College, Hammond, Ind. 46394 (A)
Catonsville Community College, Catonsville, Md.
21228 (A)
Cayuga County Community College, Auburn, N.Y.
13021 (A)
Central Missouri State University, Warrensburg, Mo.
64093 (B)
Central Ohio Technical College, Newark, Ohio
43055 (A)
Central Virginia Community College, Lynchburg,
Va. 24502 (A)
Central YMCA Community College, Chicago, Ill.
60185 (A)
Champlain College, Burlington, Vt. 05401 (A)
Charles County Community College, La Plata, Md.
20646 (A)
Clarkson College of Technology, Potsdam, N.Y.
13676 (A)
Coe College, Cedar Rapids, Iowa 52402 (A)
College of St. Catherine, St. Paul, Minn. 55105 (B)
Columbia College, Columbia, Mo. 65201 (B)
Columbia State Community College, Columbia,
Tenn. 38401 (A)
Community College of Denver, North Campus, Den-
ver, Colo. 80020 (A)
Community College of Denver, Red Rocks Campus,
Golden, Colo. 80401 (A)
DePauw University, Greencastle, Ind. 46135 (B)
Dean Junior College, Franklin, Mass. 02038 (A)

Des Moines Area Community College, Ankeny,
Iowa 50021 (A)
East Tennessee State University, Johnson City, Tenn.
37601 (B)
Eastern Illinois University, Charleston, Ill. 61920
(B)
Eastern Kentucky University, Richmond, Ky. 40475
(B)
Embry-Riddle Aeronautical University, Daytona
Beach, Fla. 32014 (B)
Grand Rapids Junior College, Grand Rapids, Mich.
49502 (A)
Grand Valley State Colleges, Allendale, Mich.
49401 (B)
High Point College, High Point, N.C. 27262 (B)
Indiana University–Purdue University, Fort Wayne,
Ind. 46805 (A)
Indiana Vocational Technical College, Indianapolis,
Ind. 46202 (A)
Indiana Vocational Technical College, South Bend,
Ind. 46619 (A)
Johnson and Wales College, Providence, R.I. 02903
(A)
Juniata College, Huntingdon, Pa. 16652 (B)
Kansas State University, Manhattan, Kans. 66506
(B)
Kentucky Wesleyan College, Owensboro, Ky. 42301
(A)
Lake Land College, Mattoon, Ill. 61938 (A)
Lawrence Institute of Technology, Southfield, Mich.
48075 (B)
Madonna College, Livonia, Mich. 48150 (A, B)

Manchester College, North Manchester, Ind. 46962
(A, B)
Manhattan College, Bronx, N.Y. 10471 (B)
Marion Military Institute, Marion, Ala. 36756 (A)
Marycrest College, Davenport, Iowa 52804 (B)
Marywood College, Scranton, Pa. 18509 (B)
McGill University, Montreal, Quebec, Canada (M)
Menlo College, Menlo Park, Calif. 94025 (A)
Merced College, Merced, Calif. 95340 (A)
Middlesex Community College, Middletown, Conn.
06457 (A)
Missouri Western State College, St. Joseph, Mo.
64507 (B)
Monterey Peninsula College, Monterey, Calif. 93940
(A)
Morehead State University, Morehead, Ky. 40351
(A)
Motlow State Community College, Tullahoma, Tenn.
37388
National College of Business, Rapid City, S. Dak.
57701 (A, B)
New Hampshire College, Manchester, N.H. 03104
(B)
New Mexico Military Institute, Roswell, N. Mex.
88201 (A)
Nicholls State University, Thibodaux, La. 70301
(A)
North Iowa Ames Community College, Mason City,
Iowa 50401 (A)
Northern Illinois University, DeKalb, Ill. 60115 (B)
Northwestern Connecticut Community College, Win-
sted, Conn. 06098 (A)

Northwestern University, Evanston, Ill. 60201 (B, M, D)

Notre Dame College of Ohio, Cleveland, Ohio 44121 (B)

Oberlin College, Oberlin, Ohio 44074 (B)

Olympic College, Bremerton, Wash. 98310 (A)

Ottawa University, Ottawa, Kans. 66067 (B)

Pace University, Pleasantville, N.Y. 10570 (B)

Palm Beach Junior College, Lake Worth, Fla. 33461 (A)

Parkersburg Community College, Parkersburg, W. Va. 26101 (A)

Pitt Technical Institute, Greenville, N.C. 27834 (A)

C. W. Post College (Long Island University), Greenvale, N.Y. 11548 (B)

Prince George's Community College, Largo, Md. 20870 (A)

Purdue University, West Lafayette, Ind. 47907 (A, B, M)

Reynolds (J. Sargeant) Community College, Richmond, Va. 23241 (A)

Robert Morris College, Coraopolis, Pa. 15108 (B)

Rochester Institute of Technology, Rochester, N.Y. 14623 (A, B, M)

St. Gregory's College, Shawnee, Okla. 74801 (A)

St. Martin's College, Olympia, Wash. 98503 (A, B)

Scott Community College, Bettendorf, Iowa 52722 (A)

Seward County Community Junior College, Liberal, Kans. 67901 (A)

Shepherd College, Shepherdstown, W. Va. 25443 (A)

Sierra College, Rocklin, Calif. 95677 (A)
Skagit Valley College, Mount Vernon, Wash. 98273
   (A)
Southeast Missouri State University, Cape Girar-
   deau, Mo. 63701 (A)
Southeastern Louisiana University, Hammond, La.
   70402 (A)
Southeastern Oklahoma State University, Durant,
   Okla. 74701 (B)
Southern Illinois University, Edwardsville, Ill. 62026
   (B)
Southern Methodist University, Dallas, Tex. 75275
   (B)
Southern University & Agricultural and Mechanical
   College, Baton Rouge, La. 70813 (B)
Southwestern at Memphis, Memphis, Tenn. 38112
   (B)
Southwestern College, Winfield, Kans. 67156
Southwestern Oklahoma State University, Weather-
   ford, Okla. 73096 (B)
Spelman College, Atlanta, Ga. 30314 (B)
Spring Garden College, Philadelphia, Pa. 19118 (A,
   B)
State University of New York, Albany, N.Y. 12222
   (M)
Stephens College, Columbia, Mo. 65201 (B)
Stockton State College, Pomona, N.J. 08239 (B)
Strayer College, Washington, D.C. 20005 (A)
Texas A & M University, College Station, Tex.
   77843 (B, M)
Texas Southern University, Houston, Tex. 77004
   (B)

Texas Southmost College, Brownsville, Tex. 78520 (A)
Thiel College, Greenville, Pa. 16125 (A)
Tri-State University, Angola, Ind. 46703
Troy State University, Troy, Ala. 36081 (B)
Tufts University, Medford, Mass. 02155 (B)
Union County Technical Institute, Scotch Plains, N.J. 07076 (A)
University of Cincinnati, Cincinnati, Ohio 45221 (A)
University of Dayton, Dayton, Ohio 45469 (B, M)
University of Evansville, Evansville, Ind. 47702 (A, B)
University of Hawaii, Leeward Community College, Pearl City, Hawaii 96782 (A)
University of Houston, Houston, Tex. 77004 (B)
University of Maine, Augusta, Maine 04330 (A)
University of Maine, Machias, Maine 04654 (A)
University of Mississippi, University, Miss. 38677 (B)
University of New Haven, West Haven, Conn. 06516 (B)
University of Toledo, Toledo, Ohio 43606 (A)
Victoria College, Victoria, Tex. 77901 (A)
Washington University, St. Louis, Mo. 63130 (B)
Wayne State University, Detroit, Mich. 48202 (B, M)
Weber State College, Ogden, Utah 84408 (A, B)
West Virginia State College, Institute, W. Va. 25122 (B)
West Virginia Wesleyan College, Buckhannon, W. Va. 26201 (B, M)

Western Kentucky University, Bowling Green, Ky.
  42101 (B)
Western Washington State College, Bellingham,
  Wash. 98225 (B)
Western Wyoming Community College, Rock Spring,
  Wyo. 82901 (A)
Westfield State College, Westfield, Mass. 01085 (B)
Wilkes College, Wilkes-Barre, Pa. 18703 (B)
Winona State University, Winona, Minn. 55987 (B)

Systems analysts plan efficient procedures for processing data. They analyze complicated business and scientific problems and then formulate programmable data-processing systems. Systems analysts prepare instructions for the computer programmers and then test the functioning of the systems. The systems they devise process information to solve miscellaneous business, engineering, and scientific problems. These problems may range from monitoring nuclear fission in a powerplant to forecasting seasonal resort-hotel reservations.

Only about 10 percent of the systems analysts are women. As with the computer programmers, there are no specific educational requirements for positions as systems analysts. Generally, experience in computer programming is required. Preference is given to those who are college graduates. Backgrounds in accounting, business, and/or economics are desirable for employment in banks or other financial institutions; backgrounds in the physical and biological sciences, mathematics, and/or engineering are desirable for employment in engineering concerns, hospitals, institutions, medical research, and/or scientifically oriented organizations.

Some employers prefer to hire as systems analysts those who have graduate degrees in computer science and systems analysis. All require that those who seek these positions should have the ability to concentrate and think logically and should like to work with ideas.

Following are the names and addresses of institutions of higher education that offer four- and more year degree programs in *systems analysis* leading to bachelor's, master's, and doctor's degrees, with the B, M, and D indicating the specific degree program(s) offered:

Arizona State University, Tempe, Ariz. 85281 (B)
Baptist College, Charleston, S.C. 29411 (B)
Baruch (Bernard M.) College, City University of
    New York, New York, N.Y. 10010 (B, M)
Baylor University, Waco, Tex. 76706 (B, M)
Boston University, Boston, Mass. 02215 (B)
Bowling Green State University, Bowling Green,
    Ohio 43403 (B)
Bradley University, Peoria, Ill. 61625 (B, M)
Brigham Young University, Provo, Utah 84602 (B,
    M)
Brown University, Providence, R.I. 02912 (B, M,
    D)
Bryant College, Smithfield, R.I. 02917 (B)
Butler University, Indianapolis, Ind. 46208 (B)
California State University, Fresno, Calif. 93740 (B)
California State University, Fullerton, Calif. 92634
    (B, M)
Carnegie-Mellon University, Pittsburgh, Pa. 15213
    (M, D)
Central College, Pella, Iowa 50219 (B)

Coe College, Cedar Rapids, Iowa 52402 (B)

DePauw University, Greencastle, Ind. 46135 (B)

Eastern Washington State College, Cheney, Wash. 99004 (B)

Elmira College, Elmira, N.Y. 14901 (B)

Evergreen State College, Olympia, Wash. 98505 (B)

Fairleigh Dickinson University, Teaneck-Hackensack Campus, Teaneck, N.J. 07666 (M)

Ferris State College, Big Rapids, Mich. 49307 (B)

Florida Institute of Technology, Melbourne, Fla. 32901 (M)

Georgia Southern College, Statesboro, Ga. 30458 (B)

Georgia Southwestern College, Americus, Ga. 31709 (B)

Gonzaga University, Spokane, Wash. 99258 (B)

Harvard College, Cambridge, Mass. 01778 (B)

Indiana University of Pennsylvania, Indiana, Pa. 15701 (B)

Johnson and Wales College, Providence, R.I. 02903 (B)

Juniata College, Huntingdon, Pa. 16652 (B)

Kansas State University, Manhattan, Kans. 66506 (B, M, D)

Knox College, Galesburg, Ill. 61401 (B)

Madonna College, Livonia, Mich. 48150 (B)

Mankato State University, Mankato, Minn. 56001 (B, M)

Marycrest College, Davenport, Iowa 52804 (B)

Marygrove College, Detroit, Mich. 48221 (B)

Marywood College, Scranton, Pa. 18509 (B)

McGill University, Montreal, Quebec, Canada (M)

Miami University, Oxford, Ohio 45056 (B)
Michigan Technological University, Houghton, Mich. 49931 (B)
Middle Tennessee State University, Murfreesboro, Tenn. 37132 (B)
National College of Business, Rapid City, S. Dak. 57701 (B)
New Hampshire College, Manchester, N.H. 03104 (B)
New Mexico State University, Las Cruces, N. Mex. 88003 (B, M)
New York University, New York, N.Y. 10003 (B, M)
Northern Illinois University, DeKalb, Ill. 60115 (B)
Northwestern University, Evanston, Ill. 60201 (B, M, D)
Polytechnic Institute of New York, Brooklyn, N.Y. 11201 (B, M, D)
Pomona College, Claremont, Calif. 91711 (B)
Pratt Institute, Brooklyn, N.Y. 11205 (B)
Purdue University, West Lafayette, Ind. 47907 (B, M, D)
Radcliffe College, Cambridge, Mass. 01778 (B)
Robert Morris College, Coraopolis, Pa. 15108 (B)
Rochester Institute of Technology, Rochester, N.Y. 14623 (B, M)
Rockhurst College, Kansas City, Mo. 64110 (B)
St. Joseph's College, Rensselaer, Ind. 47978 (B)
Shepherd College, Shepherdstown, W. Va. 25443 (B)

Southern Methodist University, Dallas, Tex. 75275 (B)
State University of New York, Stony Brook, N.Y. 11794 (M, D)
Stevens Institute of Technology, Hoboken, N.J. 07030 (B, M, D)
Stockton State College, Pomona, N.J. 08239 (B)
Strayer College, Washington, D.C. 20005 (B)
Susquehanna University, Selinsgrove, Pa. 17870 (B)
Taylor University, Upland, Ind. 46989 (B)
Texas Christian University, Fort Worth, Tex. 76129 (M)
Tri-State University, Angola, Ind. 46703 (B)
Tufts University, Medford, Mass. 02155 (B)
University of California at San Diego, La Jolla, Calif. 92093 (B, D)
University of Cincinnati, Cincinnati, Ohio 45221 (B, M)
University of Colorado, Denver, Colo. 80202 (M)
University of Detroit, Detroit, Mich. 48221 (B)
University of Georgia, Athens, Ga. 30602 (B, M, D)
University of Illinois at Chicago Circle, Chicago, Ill. 60680 (B, M)
University of Maryland, College Park, Md. 20742 (M, D)
University of Miami, Coral Gables, Fla. 33124 (B, M)
University of New Haven, West Haven, Conn. 06516 (B)
University of Southern California, Los Angeles, Calif. 90007 (M)

University of Texas, Austin, Tex. 78712 (D)
University of Toledo, Toledo, Ohio 43606 (B)
University of Vermont, Burlington, Vt. 05401 (B)
University of Virginia, Charlottesville, Va. 22903 (B, M, D)
Washington University, St. Louis, Mo. 63130 (B, M, D)
Wayne State University, Detroit, Mich. 48202 (B, M)
West Coast University, Los Angeles, Calif. 90020 (M)
Western Washington State College, Bellingham, Wash. 98225 (B)
Wilkes College, Wilkes-Barre, Pa. 18703 (B)
Worcester Polytechnic Institute, Worcester, Mass. 01609 (B, M)

It is anticipated that the use of computers will expand rapidly throughout the 1980s and consequently the demand for computer-operating personnel, computer programmers, and systems analysts will continue to rise. Employment opportunities are expected to be excellent and to grow faster in this industry than the average for all occupations.

Expanding computer usage will take place in all areas of business, industry, and scientifically oriented organizations, and especially so in medical, educational, and data-processing services.

For further information about career opportunities in the computer industry, write to: American Federation of Information Processing Societies, 210 Summit Ave., Montvale, N.J. 07645.

6
People, People Everywhere—
Growing Older Every Year

Demography is the study and science of social and vital statistics. It is a new branch of the field of applied statistics.

Specifically, demography is the study of populations and the births, marriages, divorces, diseases, deaths, and a miscellany of other changes and characteristics of populations. The migration of people from one location to another, the number of children in families in a particular area, the aging of the population, and the number of people who are single, married, divorced, or widowed are among the characteristics considered in demographic studies.

The *demographer* is the specialist in the field of demography. Demographers are also known as *populations specialists* and *demography statisticians.* They plan and conduct varied surveys, censuses, and experiments in order to collect statistics concerning human populations. After obtaining these statistics, they analyze them to help government, business officials, educators, and others to plan for the future. The statistics they gather about populations may include age, economic status, family structure, race, sex, and size of these populations.

Demographic studies help involved officials to determine whether or not new schools, hospitals, and homes for the aged will be needed in certain locations in the future. These studies also aid businessmen to establish new products and new markets.

How many babies were born last year? Was the number less or greater than the previous year? What can be done to bring about changes in the growth of populations? Where does zero population growth exist? Which illnesses and disorders are causing people to be hospitalized? Are the people in the city under study living to an older age? How many are in their seventies and their eighties? How many people died last year and of what causes? Which age and ethnic groups will purchase a new product and where are these groups located? All of these are questions to which demographers seek the answers.

The demographers figure out the number of new homes and housing projects which should be built to meet the needs of shifts in populations. They determine the manpower potentials in a given area and whether labor force needs could be met. They gather information about the area wherein specific ethnic groups are concentrated. Their studies are designed to improve life and living conditions in the present and the future. These studies enable them to point out existing problems, so that action can be taken to arrest and rectify these problems.

Changes in populations are affected by many conditions, including biological, economic, environmental, psychological, and social conditions. Thus, to analyze the results of these studies realistically, demographers need training in, and understanding of, these subjects as well as statistics.

Most demographers are employed by colleges and universities, where they teach and do research. The next largest group works for government agencies and business concerns. Others are employed by international organizations, such as the Population Division of the United Nations and the World Health Organization.

Demography is so young a field that there are few undergraduate-major programs leading to the bachelor's degree in demography. Those who are interested in careers as demographers, if they do not attend a college that offers major study in demography, should major in sociology or statistics, including courses in anthropology, ecology, economics, government, population, and urban affairs.

Following are the names and addresses of institutions of higher education that offer four- and more year degree programs in *demography,* leading to bachelor's, master's, and doctor's degrees, with the B, M, and D indicating the specific degree program(s) offered:

Bennington College, Bennington, Vt. 05201 (B)
Brown University, Providence, R.I. 02912 (M, D)
California State College, Dominguez Hills, Calif. 90747 (B)
Columbia College (Columbia University), New York, N.Y. 10027 (B)
Cornell University, Ithaca, N.Y. 14853 (M, D)
Georgetown University, Washington, D.C. 20057 (M)

Northwestern University, Evanston, Ill. 60201 (M)
Princeton University, Princeton, N.J. 08540 (D)
State University of New York, Empire State College,
   Saratoga Springs, N.Y. 12866 (B)
University of California, Berkeley, Calif. 94720 (D)
University of Chicago, Chicago, Ill. 60637 (M, D)
University of Colorado, Denver, Colo. 80202 (B)
University of Montana, Missoula, Mont. 59812 (B,
   M)
University of Pennsylvania, Philadelphia, Pa. 19104
   (B, M, D)

Would you like additional information about the field of demography? If so, write to the Population Association of America, Inc., P.O. Box 14182, Benjamin Franklin Station, Washington, D.C. 20044.

Demographic studies have shown that approximately 21 million Americans are past the age of sixty-five. By the year 2000, it is anticipated that this number shall have risen to about 30 million and by the year 2020 to about 40 million. If heart disease and cancer are conquered before that time, these numbers will be even greater than now anticipated.

In 1978, there were about 8.5 million Americans over the age of seventy-five. This number is expected to jump to 13.5 million by the year 2000. The elderly are considered to be the fastest growing population group in the United States. The members of this group have the greatest need for health and social services.

The word "gerontology" is derived from the Greek

"geronto," which means "old age." Gerontology means the study of aging and the special problems of older people. In 1977, more than one million people were employed in the field of gerontology, the field of aging. More than 75 percent of them were working in institutions broadly classified as "nursing homes," including public and private homes for the aged, convalescent homes, and miscellaneous extended-care facilities. Many were working in federally funded programs and services that had been established as a result of the Older Americans Act of 1965.

Since this original act of 1965, there has been an increase in federal-government allocations for programs to aid the aged. As a result of this and the rapidly increasing growth of this population group, the field of gerontology has blossomed. Although many of the needs of the elderly are being met by the traditional nurses and social workers, a great many of their special needs and problems call for the services of a unique, new professional, the *gerontology specialist.*

It is these gerontology specialists who will be trained to be specifically responsive to the particular problems that beset older people. These specialists are also known as *gerontologists* or by the title of the more specific functions performed, such as *home health aides, nursing-home directors, retirement-home administrators, senior-center directors, social planners,* and *therapeutic-recreation specialists.*

Gerontology is so new that just a few years back it was unheard of as a course, or subject, on American college campuses. Now, courses in gerontology are being offered in many colleges and universities throughout the land.

Often they are included in the health education, nursing, psychology, or sociology departments. Additionally, a small but growing number of institutions of higher education are offering major study programs in gerontology. These major programs include courses covering the economic, legal, leisure, nutritional, personal, psychological, sexual, and social problems of the aged.

The pioneering university in this field has been the University of Southern California with its Ethel Perry Andrus Gerontology Center (University Park, Los Angeles, Calif. 90007). Undergraduate and graduate programs are offered here to help meet the special needs of the elderly residents of the greater Los Angeles area. All too often, loss of memory is a tragic accompaniment of old age. This Center has a Memory Clinic aimed at helping elderly people with memory problems; students are also taught how to aid the aging in improving their memory.

The California State College (Dominguez Hills) also offers a comprehensive program in gerontology. Courses are offered in such subjects as applied gerontology, counseling, health care, human services, nutrition, psychology, and sociology. This program also includes a supervised internship in which students devote six hundred hours to working with the aged in a community, nursing, or other setting.

In addition to California State University and the University of Southern California, degree programs in gerontology are offered by the following institutions of higher education:

Boston University, Boston, Mass. 02215
Duke University, Durham, N.C. 27706
Florida State University, Tallahassee, Fla. 32306
Illinois State University, Normal, Ill. 61761
Miami University, Oxford, Ohio 45056
Michigan State University, East Lansing, Mich. 48824
Pennsylvania State University, University Park, Pa. 16802
Portland State University, Portland, Oreg. 97207
St. Louis University, St. Louis, Mo. 63103
San Diego State University, San Diego, Calif. 92182
University of South Florida, Tampa, Fla. 33620
Utah State University, Logan, Utah 84322

Some institutions of higher education offer concentrations in gerontology via interdisciplinary programs. The students take miscellaneous gerontology courses in such departments as home economics, psychology, sociology, and urban planning. The biological, psychological, and social aspects of aging involve several different academic disciplines. Thus, the home economics department may offer a "Nutritional Problems of the Aging" course, the psychology department may offer "Loneliness among the Aged," the sociology department may offer "Social Crises in Aging," and the urban planning department may offer "Housing for the Elderly."

There is a great demand and need for those trained in gerontology. With the passage of time, this need will intensify. The services required by the elderly are many, and those who are trained and qualified to provide these services should find ample employment opportunities.

The number of older Americans is increasing rapidly and they are becoming a more vocal group demanding the services to which they are entitled.

Career opportunities in the field of aging are so diverse that many enter this field with varied academic backgrounds. It is best, however, for candidates for positions to have training in gerontology, plus a genuine desire to help and work with the aged. It is also advisable for students to do volunteer work in this field to determine whether or not it is one for which they are well suited.

In the field of nursing, a gerontological specialty has been established. The American Nurses Association (ANA) has sponsored courses on the fundamentals of gerontological nursing since 1973 and thousands of registered nurses have taken these courses. *Gerontological nurses* should have a knowledge of the aging process. Nurses who pass an ANA-certification-board written examination, demonstrate excellence in clinical practice, and receive the required endorsement by their colleagues may be certified as gerontological nurses.

It is anticipated that the employment outlook in the field of gerontology will be bright throughout the 1980s, especially for positions with service programs such as: (*a*) community services—counseling, education, health, information and referral, recreation, and transportation services offered at senior centers and varied public and private agencies; (*b*) home services—assistance to people who are confined to their homes and may have problems caring for themselves; (*c*) housing—special facilities and projects to meet the needs of the elderly at a price they can afford to pay; (*d*) legal services dealing with special problems of the aged, such as matters pertaining to pensions, taxes, wills, Medicaid, Medicare, and Social Security; (*e*) nutrition programs, including home-delivered meals, and (*f*) nursing homes—for the care of the most frail and most vulnerable among the aged.

Employment opportunities will also be available with federal, state, and local agencies that coordinate, plan, and evaluate services for the elderly. Those who also have received training in recreation will be in demand to help senior citizens use their leisure time wisely and live more satisfying lives. Those who have management ability and training in administration of gerontological facilities may become housing managers, nursing-home administrators, or senior-center directors.

If you would like to obtain further information about career and training opportunities in any aspect of the broad field of gerontology, write to one or more of the following:

American Association of Homes for the Aging
1050 Seventeenth St. N.W.
Washington, D.C. 20036

American Health Care Association
1200 Fifteenth St. N.W.
Washington, D.C. 20005

National Council for Homemaker–Home Health
    Aide Services, Inc.
67 Irving Place
New York, N.Y. 10003

National Institute of Senior Citizens
National Council on the Aging
1828 L St. N.W.
Washington, D.C. 20036

National Therapeutic Recreation Society
1601 North Kent
Arlington, Va. 22209

U.S. Department of Health, Education and Welfare
Office of Human Development
National Clearinghouse on Aging
Administration on Aging
Washington, D.C. 20201

U.S. Department of Housing and Urban Development
Office of Housing Management
451 Seventh St. N.W.
Washington, D.C. 20024

Allied to the field of gerontology is the field of *geriatrics*. Geriatrics is the medical specialty that deals with the diseases and disorders of the aged. It is one of the newest of the medical specialties. Just as there is a specialty known as pediatrics, which deals with the diseases and disorders of children, so, now, at the other end of the age scale, there is geriatrics.

Although their number is still small, an increasing number of physicians are becoming *geriatricians*. As with gerontologists, the demand for geriatricians will grow as life expectancy increases.

In January 1978, the Veterans Administration announced that it was setting up training programs in geriatrics for VA physicians. More than 13 million veterans of World War II are in, or close to, their sixties, and the Veterans Administration is eager to have physicians who are qualified to tend to the specific health problems of these older veterans. The two-year training program in geriatrics was begun in the VA hospitals in Little Rock, Ark.; Los Angeles, Calif.; Palo Alto, Calif.; Lexington, Ky.; Bedford, Mass.; and Philadelphia, Pa.

If you aspire to becoming a physician and think you might like to specialize in geriatrics, write to the American Medical Association, 535 N. Dearborn St., Chicago, Ill. 60610, for further information about this specialty.

7
New Caring Health Careers

Nursing is an ancient profession, but within it some new careers are emerging. The *gerontological nurse* has already been mentioned in Chapter 6. The *nurse-midwife* is another such new career.

Certified nurse-midwives (*C.N.M.*) are registered nurses who have completed advanced study and obtained clinical experience in obstetric care. A pregnant woman may be placed under the care of a certified nurse-midwife after the obstetrician has determined that all signs point toward a normal pregnancy. Thus, nurse-midwives manage the care of pregnant women whose physical examinations and medical histories indicate that their pregnancies will in all probability be normal. The nurse-midwives are involved in the care of these women throughout the entire maternity cycle. They deliver babies and continue to care for the mothers and their babies until the babies become one year of age.

Nurse-midwives do not work as independent practitioners. They work as members of obstetric teams in cooperation with physicians and other nurses. However, they are capable of assuming responsibility for the total care of healthy pregnant women. They offer physical and emotional support to expectant mothers throughout the pregnancy, during labor, and thereafter.

The nurse-midwives examine the patients regularly and monitor all stages of labor. If they note any deviation from normality, they immediately contact the obstetrician-gynecologist. Nurse-midwives give newborn babies their first physical examinations. They educate and counsel mothers on all aspects of child care. They also plan community health-education programs and offer counseling in family planning.

Registered nurses who would like to become nurse-midwives must complete an approved program at a school of nurse-midwifery. Following are programs approved by the American College of Nurse-Midwives:

Booth Maternity Center, Philadelphia, Pa. 19131

College of Medicine and Dentistry of New Jersey, School of Allied Health Professions, Nurse-Midwifery Program, Newark, N.J. 07103

Columbia University–Presbyterian Medical Center, Graduate Program in Maternity Nursing and Nurse-Midwifery, New York, N.Y. 10032

Frontier School of Midwifery and Family Nursing, Wendover, Ky. 41775

Georgetown University School of Nursing, Washington, D.C. 20007

Johns Hopkins University, School of Hygiene and Public Health, Nurse-Midwifery Program, Baltimore, Md. 21205

Medical University of South Carolina, Nurse-Midwifery Program, Charleston, S.C. 29401

St. Louis University, Department of Nursing, Graduate Program in Nurse-Midwifery, St. Louis, Mo. 63104

Simpson Center for Maternal Health, Community Hospital of Springfield and Clark County, Springfield, Ohio 45505

State University of New York, Downstate Medical Center, College of Health Related Professions, Nurse-Midwifery Program, Brooklyn, N.Y. 11203

U.S. Air Force, Malcolm Grow Medical Center, Nurse-Midwifery Program, Andrews Air Force Base, Md. 20331

University of Illinois Medical Center, College of Nursing, Nurse-Midwifery Program, Chicago, Ill. 60680

University of Kentucky, Chandler Medical Center, Lexington, Ky. 40506

University of Mississippi, Nurse-Midwifery Program, Jackson, Miss. 39216

University of Utah, College of Nursing, Salt Lake City, Utah 84112

Yale University, School of Nursing, New Haven, Conn. 16510

Applicants for admission to these programs must be registered nurses. Some of the programs additionally require the bachelor's degree for admission and lead to the master's degree; others call for only the R.N. and lead to a certificate upon completion of the program. The master's degree program may range in length from one to two years. The certificate program ranges from nine months to one year in length. Graduates of these programs must pass the American College of Nurse-Midwives certification examination in order to be approved as a "certified nurse-midwife."

In 1977, there were approximately two thousand certified nurse-midwives. This number is expected to grow rapidly as more states permit nurse-midwives to practice fully. Nurses who find obstetric care attractive should find excellent employment opportunities available to them.

If you would like additional information about training and career opportunities in nurse-midwifery, write to the American College of Nurse-Midwifery, Suite 1200, 1000 Vermont Ave. N.W., Washington, D.C. 20005.

Breathing is vital to life. We need oxygen to live. If a person stops breathing for more than three to five minutes, brain damage generally follows. If breathing ceases and oxygen is not available for more than nine minutes, death is the general result.

There are new careerists whose function essentially is to come to the rescue when patients have breathing difficulties. These are the *inhalation-therapy workers.* They are known too as *respiratory-therapy workers.* These workers include the *inhalation therapists, inhalation-therapy technicians,* and *inhalation-therapy assistants* (also known as *respiratory therapists, respiratory technicians,* and *respiratory assistants*). The therapists and technicians perform basically the same functions. The therapists, however, have a higher level of expertise and may also have some supervisory tasks. The inhalation-therapy assistants have little, if any, contact with patients; they generally take care of the respiration equipment.

Inhalation therapists and inhalation-therapy technicians treat patients with cardiorespiratory (breathing) problems and play essential roles in emergencies. Their work may range from administering temporary relief to asthmatic patients to giving emergency treatment in cases of heart failure and stroke. They follow the physicians' orders and employ special equipment such as respirators and other respiration-treatment machines. They may also instruct patients and members of their families on the use of such equipment at home.

Respiration therapists and technicians need mechanical dexterity to operate the respiration equipment. Inability to breathe is a very frightening experience and, therefore, these workers should have an understanding of the psychological, as well as the physical, needs of their patients.

In this very young occupation, workers in the early 1970s were trained in the hospitals on the job. Today, however, inhalation therapists and inhalation-therapy technicians must be high school graduates who have completed an approved inhalation-therapy program.

Those who have completed a therapist training program approved by the American Medical Association, two years of college, and one year of experience after graduation from the approved program, may apply to take the registry examination of the National Board for Respiratory Therapy. Upon passing this examination, they are awarded the American Registered Respiratory Therapist (ARRT) credential. Those who complete a technician-training program approved by the American

Medical Association, followed by one year of experience, may take the examination for the Certified Respiratory Therapy Technician (CRTT) credential.

There are still no formal requirements for the position of respiratory-therapy assistant; in the main, high school graduates hired for these positions are given on-the-job training.

Following are the names and addresses of institutions of higher education that offer two-year associate degree programs in *inhalation-therapy technology:*

Alabama Christian College, Montgomery, Ala. 36109

American River College, Sacramento, Calif. 95841

Atlantic Community College, Mays Landing, N.J. 08330

Barton County Community College, Great Bend, Kans. 67530

Bluefield State College, Bluefield, W. Va. 24701

Boise State University, Boise, Idaho 83725

Brookdale Community College, Lincroft, N.J. 07738

Broward Community College, Fort Lauderdale, Fla. 33301

Brunswick Junior College, Brunswick, Ga. 31520

Butte College, Oroville, Calif. 95965

Calhoun (John C.) State Community College, Decatur, Ala. 35602

Central YMCA Community College, Chicago, Ill. 60185

Cleveland State Community College, Cleveland, Tenn. 37311

Clinton Community College, Clinton, Iowa 52732
Colby Community College, Colby, Kans. 67701
College of the Mainland, Texas City, Tex. 77590
College of Mount St. Joseph on the Ohio, Mount St. Joseph, Ohio 45051
College of St. Scholastica, Duluth, Minn. 55811
Columbus Technical Institute, Columbus, Ohio 43216
Community College of Baltimore, Baltimore, Md. 21215
Community College of Denver, Aurora Campus, Denver, Colo. 80204
Community College of Denver, North Campus, Denver, Colo. 80020
Cushing Junior College, Bryn Mawr, Pa. 19010
Cuyahoga Community College, Western Campus, Parma, Ohio 44130
Daytona Beach Community College, Daytona Beach, Fla. 32015
Delaware County Community College, Media, Pa. 19063
Delaware Technical and Community College, Stanton Campus. Stanton, Del. 19702
Des Moines Area Community College, Ankeny, Iowa 50021
Durham Technical Institute, Durham, N.C. 27703
El Paso Community College, El Paso, Tex. 79904
Fairleigh Dickinson University, Florham-Madison Campus, Madison, N.J. 07940
Fairmont State College, Fairmont, W. Va. 26554
Ferris State College, Big Rapids, Mich. 49307

Forsyth Technical Institute, Winston-Salem, N.C. 27103
Gadsden State Junior College, Gadsden, Ala. 35903
Georgia State University, Atlanta, Ga. 30303
Grand Rapids Junior College, Grand Rapids, Mich. 49502
Greenville Technical College, Greenville, S.C. 29606
Harrisburg Area Community College, Harrisburg, Pa. 17110
Hesston College, Hesston, Kans. 67062
Highline Community College, Midway, Wash. 98031
Hillsborough Community College, Tampa, Fla. 33622
Houston Community College, Houston, Tex. 77007
Hudson Valley Community College, Troy, N.Y. 12180
Indiana State University, Evansville, Ind. 47712
Indiana University Northwest, Gary, Ind. 46408
Indiana Vocational Technical College, Indianapolis, Ind. 46202
Kalamazoo Valley Community College, Kalamazoo, Mich. 49009
Kirkwood Community College, Cedar Rapids, Iowa, 52406
Laboure Junior College, Boston, Mass. 02124
Lamar University, Beaumont, Tex. 77710
Lane Community College, Eugene, Oreg. 97405
Lawson State Community College, Birmingham, Ala. 35211
Lincoln Land Community College, Springfield, Ill. 62708

Louisiana State University at Eunice, Eunice, La. 70535

Macomb County Community College, Center Campus, Mount Clemens, Mich. 48043

Madison Area Technical College, Madison, Wis. 53703

Manchester Community College, Manchester, Conn. 06040

Maryville College, St. Louis, Mo. 63141

Massasoit Community College, Brockton, Mass. 02402

Mercy College of Detroit, Detroit, Mich. 48219

Miami-Dade Community College, Miami, Fla. 33132

Milwaukee Area Technical College, Milwaukee, Wis. 53203

Mohawk Valley Community College, Utica, N.Y. 13501

Mount Hood Community College, Gresham, Oreg. 97030

Mount San Antonio College, Walnut, Calif. 91789

Mountain Empire Community College, Big Stone Gap, Va. 24219

Nassau Community College, Garden City, N.Y. 11530

Nebraska Wesleyan University, Lincoln, Nebr. 68504

Neosho County Community Junior College, Chanute, Kans. 66720

New Hampshire Vocational-Technical College, Claremont, N.H. 03743

North Central Michigan College, Petoskey, Mich. 49770

North Hennepin Community College, Minneapolis, Minn. 55445

North Shore Community College, Beverly, Mass. 01915

Northeast Mississippi Junior College, Booneville, Miss. 38829

Northeast Wisconsin Technical Institute, Green Bay, Wis. 54303

Northeastern University, Boston, Mass. 02115

Northern Essex Community College, Haverhill, Mass. 01830

Northern Kentucky University, Highland Heights, Ky. 41076

Northern Virginia Community College, Annandale, Va. 22151

Norwalk Community College, Norwalk, Conn. 06854

Odessa College, Odessa, Tex. 79760

Orange Coast College, Costa Mesa, Calif. 92626

Oscar Rose Junior College, Midwest City, Okla. 73110

Penn Valley Community College, Kansas City, Mo. 64111

Pensacola Junior College, Pensacola, Fla. 32504

Piedmont Virginia Community College, Charlottesville, Va. 22901

Pima Community College, Tucson, Ariz. 85709

Prince George's Community College, Largo, Md. 20870

Quinnipiac College, Hamden, Conn. 06518

Rhode Island Junior College, Warwick, R.I. 02886
Rochester Community College, Rochester, Minn. 55901
St. Mary's Junior College, Minneapolis, Minn. 55454
St. Petersburg Junior College, St. Petersburg, Fla. 33733
St. Philip's College, San Antonio, Tex. 78203
Santa Monica College, Santa Monica, Calif. 90405
Santa Rosa Junior College, Santa Rosa, Calif. 95401
Seattle Central Community College, Seattle, Wash. 98122
Shenandoah College, Winchester, Va. 22601
Sinclair Community College, Dayton, Ohio 45402
Sioux Falls College, Sioux Falls, S. Dak. 57101
Skyline College, San Bruno, Calif. 94066
South Plains College, Levelland, Tex. 79336
Southeast Community College, Lincoln, Nebr. 68501
Southwest Missouri State University, Springfield, Mo. 65802
Spokane Community College, Spokane, Wash. 99207
Springfield Technical Community College, Springfield, Mass. 01105
State Fair Community College, Sedalia, Mo. 65301
Tarrant County Junior College, Fort Worth, Tex. 76102
Temple Junior College, Temple, Tex. 76501
Trident Technical College, Charleston, S.C. 29411
Triton College, River Grove, Ill. 60171
Union County Technical Institute, Scotch Plains, N.J. 07076
University of Akron, Akron, Ohio 44325

University of Albuquerque, Albuquerque, N. Mex. 87140
University of Toledo, Toledo, Ohio 43606
Vincennes University, Vincennes, Ind. 47591
Volunteer State Community College, Gallatin, Tenn. 37066
Washtenaw Community College, Ann Arbor, Mich. 48106
Weber State College, Ogden, Utah 84408
Wenatchee Valley College, Wenatchee, Wash. 98801
Westchester Community College, Valhalla, N.Y. 10595
West Virginia Northern Community College, Wheeling, W. Va. 26003
York College of Pennsylvania, York, Pa. 17405

It is expected that employment opportunities for inhalation-therapy workers will be very good throughout the 1980s. For further information about training and career opportunities in this field, write to the American Association for Respiratory Therapy, 7411 Hines Place, Dallas, Tex. 75235, and the National Board for Respiratory Therapy, Inc., 1900 West 47th St., Westwood, Kans. 66205.

Some years back, when young medical-school graduates entered upon their hospital internships, they devoted part of these internships to ambulance duty. Today, hospital interns spend all of their time treating patients inside the hospitals and rarely, if ever, go out to do ambulance duty.

There followed a period of time when ambulance drivers were trained in first aid and they attempted, as best they could, to take the place of the young physicians. Now, the new occupation of *emergency medical technician,* at times known as *ambulance attendant,* has arisen.

Emergency medical technicians play vital roles in providing emergency medical services. They generally work in teams of two, one driving the ambulance and the other inside the ambulance with the patient(s). They are dispatched to all sorts of emergencies, including automobile and other accidents, heart attacks, wounds from shootings. When they arrive at the scene of the emergency, they must determine the nature and extent of the problem and administer appropriate emergency medical care. They may find it necessary to perform such immediate functions as controlling bleeding, restoring breathing, immobilizing fractures, assisting in childbirth, and providing initial care to burn and poison victims.

These technicians strap the patients onto stretchers, place them in the ambulance, and secure the stretchers inside to insure a safe journey to the nearest hospital best equipped for the needs of the specific patient. On the way to the hospital, the emergency medical technicians are in radio communication with the hospital emergency-room physician. They inform the physician of the extent and nature of the illness or injuries so that all is in readiness when the ambulance arrives at the hospital. They assist in transferring the patient(s) from the ambulance into the hospital emergency room and may, if necessary, help the emergency-room staff.

Those who would like to become emergency medical technicians must be at least eighteen years of age, have a high school diploma and a valid driver's license, and complete a standard eighty-one-hour training program designed by the U.S. Department of Transportation. This program is offered by fire, health and police departments; it is also offered in many hospitals, medical schools, colleges and universities. Those who successfully complete these training programs, and also comply with the experience requirements, may take the examination administered by the National Registry of Emergency Medical Technicians. If they pass this examination, they are awarded the title of Registered EMT-Ambulance.

The training given to emergency medical technicians emphasizes the importance of exercising good judgment and acting with efficiency and confidence to reduce the patient's trauma. These technicians work under very difficult conditions and, therefore, must be in good health, emotionally stable, and capable of adapting to stressful situations.

The public has begun to demand more and better emergency medical services. It is anticipated that this demand will grow, the need for emergency medical technicians will increase, and employment opportunities for these technicians will be excellent throughout the 1980s.

If you would like to find out where in your locality you may take an EMT-training program, write to the Emergency Medical Services Division of the Health Department of your state.

For additional information about career opportunities and registration for emergency medical technicians, write to Emergency Medical Services Branch, National Highway Traffic Safety Administration, 400 Seventh St. S.W., Washington, D.C. 20590, and the National Registry of Emergency Medical Technicians, 1395 East Dublin-Granville Road, P. O. Box 29233, Columbus, Ohio 43229.

8
Careers in the Creative-Arts Therapies

The three major creative-arts therapies are art therapy, dance therapy, and music therapy. These are new and emerging professions in the field of mental health.

The *art therapists, dance therapists,* and *music therapists* use their specific disciplines to aid in the care and treatment of children and adults who have learning disabilities or who may be emotionally disturbed, mentally ill, mentally retarded, physically disabled, or socially maladjusted. They all work in cooperation with the physicians and other professional members of the rehabilitation and therapeutic teams at hospitals, clinics, psychiatric institutions, community mental-health centers, nursing homes, halfway houses, schools, prisons, and miscellaneous other institutions.

The *creative-arts therapists* serve a population ranging in age from young children to geriatric patients.

Art therapists help patients express themselves via drawings, paintings, and/or clay sculpture. They employ arts as a means of fostering personal growth and self-awareness and of coping with emotional conflicts. These therapists offer patients opportunities for self-expression via the art medium. Patients thus can express their feelings and bring out their inner turmoils through art work.

Art therapy like the other creative-arts therapies is a young profession. The American Art Therapy Association, dedicated essentially to "the progressive development of the therapeutic use of art," was founded in 1969. This association has encouraged the development of professional training programs, and as a result, the number of bachelor's and master's degree programs in art therapy has been growing.

Those who aspire to careers in art therapy must have art aptitude plus a keen desire to help those who are ill. Since this is such a young profession, completion of a bachelor's degree program in art therapy, which combines training in fine arts and the behavioral sciences, is generally quite sufficient for entry positions. For advancement and professional status, the master's degree is required. Those who meet the professional standards established by the American Art Therapy Association may be awarded a certificate of registration and may place the initials "ATR" and the title "Registered Art Therapist" after their names.

Following are the names and addresses of institutions of higher education that offer four- and more year degree programs in *art therapy* leading to bachelor's and master's degrees, with the B and M indicating the specific degree program(s) offered:

Albert Magnus College, New Haven, Conn. 06511 (B)
Anna Maria College, Paxton, Mass. 01612 (B)
Avila College, Kansas City, Mo. 64145 (B)

Buffalo State University College, Buffalo, N.Y. 14222 (M)
California State University, Sacramento, Calif. 95819 (M)
Capital University, Columbus, Ohio 43209 (B)
College of New Rochelle, New Rochelle, N.Y. 10801 (B, M)
College of St. Teresa, Winona, Minn. 55987 (B)
Drake University, Des Moines, Iowa 50311 (B)
Edgecliff College, Cincinnati, Ohio 45206 (B)
Edinboro State College, Edinboro, Pa. 16444 (B)
Emporia State University, Emporia, Kans. 66801 (M)
Eureka College, Eureka, Ill. 61530 (B)
Fort Hays Kansas State College, Hays, Kans. 67601 (B)
George Washington University, Washington, D.C. 20052 (M)
Goddard College, Plainfield, Vt. 05667 (M)
Hahnemann Medical College, Philadelphia, Pa. 19102 (M)
Hofstra University, Hempstead, N.Y. 11550 (M)
Immaculate Heart College, Los Angeles, Calif. 90027 (M)
Lake Erie College, Painesville, Ohio 44077 (B)
Lesley College Graduate School of Education, Cambridge, Mass. 02138 (M)
Lindenwood College, St. Louis, Mo. 65108 (M)
Lone Mountain College, San Francisco, Calif. 94118 (M)
Marian College, Indianapolis, Ind. 46222 (B)
Maryville College, St. Louis, Mo. 63141 (B)

Massachusetts College of Art, Boston, Mass. 02115
(M)
Mount Mary College, Milwaukee, Wis. 53222 (B)
New York University, New York, N.Y. 10003 (B,
M)
Pittsburg State University, Pittsburg, Kans. 66762
(B)
Pratt Institute, Brooklyn, N.Y. 11205 (M)
Ramapo College, Mahwah, N.J. 07430 (B)
St. Thomas Aquinas College, Sparkhill, N.J. 10972
(B)
Springfield College, Springfield, Mass. 01109 (B)
Temple University, Philadelphia, Pa. 19140 (M)
Trenton State College, Trenton, N.J. 08625 (B)
University of Bridgeport, Bridgeport, Conn. 06602
(B)
University of Evansville, Evansville, Ind. 44702 (B)
University of Houston at Clear Lake City, Houston,
Tex. 77058 (M)
University of Louisville, Louisville, Ky. 40208 (M)
University of Miami, Coral Gables, Fla. 33124 (B)
University of Texas, Arlington, Tex. 76010 (M)
William James College, Grand Valley State Col-
leges, Allendale, Mich. 49401 (B)
William Woods College, Fulton, Mo. 65251 (B)
Wright State University, Dayton, Ohio 45431 (M)
Xavier University of Louisiana, New Orleans, La.
70125 (B)

If you would like additional information about careers
in art therapy, write to the American Art Therapy Association, Inc., P. O. Box 11604, Pittsburg, Pa. 15228.

Many *dance therapists* would like to be known as *movement therapists* and their field to be known as movement therapy. However, their professional association is the American Dance Therapy Association, and it appears that the terms "dance therapists" and "dance therapy" are prevailing.

Dance therapy is defined as "the psychotherapeutic use of movement as a process which furthers the emotional and physical integration of the individual." It uses dance and movement interaction as a basis of aiding people with mental, emotional, social, and/or physical problems.

Dance therapists must be skilled in the art of dance and knowledgeable about psychology and the nature of mental and emotional disorders. Dance here is used as a treatment modality within the total context of the patient's therapeutic programs; this, therefore, differs from dance as employed in recreational and educational programs. Dance therapists utilize movements as a means of intervention. They focus on this nonverbal aspect of behavior.

The American Dance Therapy Association was founded in 1966 and has aimed to establish standards of competence in the field of dance therapy. It encourages the development of graduate-level dance-therapy programs. Dance therapists must meet specific professional standards to qualify for registration as a dance therapist. Those who qualify and receive the Registry Certificate may use the title "Registered Dance Therapist" and the initials "D.T.R." after their name.

The American Dance Therapy Association recommends a liberal arts program with emphasis in psychology and extensive training in a variety of dance forms, with courses in theory, improvisation, choreography, and kinesiology as undergraduate training in preparation for graduate study in dance therapy. Master's degree programs in dance therapy are considered the professional training in this field.

Following are the names and addresses of the institutions of higher education that offer four- and more year degree programs in *dance therapy,* leading to bachelor's and master's degrees, with the B and M indicating the specific degree program(s) offered:

American University, Washington, D.C. 20016 (B)
Antioch–New England Graduate School, Keene, N.H. 03431 (M)
Goucher College, Towson, Md. 21215 (B, M)
Hahnemann Medical College, Philadelphia, Pa. 19102 (M)
Hunter College (City University of New York), New York, N.Y. 10021 (M)
Immaculate Heart College, Los Angeles, Calif. 90027 (M)
Lesley College Graduate School of Education, Cambridge, Mass. 02138 (M)
Lone Mountain College, San Francisco, Calif. 94118 (M)
Marygrove College, Detroit, Mich. 48203 (B)
New York University, New York, N.Y. 10003 (B, M)
Northeastern Illinois University, Chicago, Ill. 60625 (B, M)

University of California at Los Angeles, Los Angeles, Calif. 90024 (M)
University of Wisconsin, Madison, Wis. 53706 (B)

For further information about careers in dance therapy, write to the American Dance Therapy Association, 2000 Century Plaza, Columbia, Md. 21044.

Music therapy employs music to achieve therapeutic aims. These aims are to restore, maintain and improve the mental and physical health of the patients with whom the *music therapists* work.

Music therapists, as members of the therapeutic team, plan and carry out specific musical activities based on the individual patient's needs and problems. Music therapists apply music in a therapeutic environment to help patients adjust more wholesomely to the particular society in which they live. They must be knowledgeable not only about the subject of music, but also about the theory and practice of music therapy, psychology, rehabilitation, and sociology.

Like the other creative-arts therapies, music therapy too is an emerging profession. The National Association for Music Therapy, Inc., has as its purpose "the progressive development of the therapeutic use of music in hospital, educational, and community settings." It has set up standards for the registration of music therapists. Those who meet the criteria for such registration may use the title "Registered Music Therapist" and place the initials "RMT" after their names.

Following are the names and addresses of institutions of higher education that offer four- and more year degree programs in *music therapy,* leading to bachelor's and master's degrees, with the B and M indicating the specific degree program(s) offered:

Alverno College, Milwaukee, Wis. 53215 (B)
Anna Marie College, Paxton, Mass. 01612 (B)
Arizona State University, Tempe, Ariz. 85281 (B)
Augsburg College, Minneapolis, Minn. 55404 (B)
Baptist College at Charleston, Charleston, S.C. 29411 (B)
California State University, Long Beach, Calif. 90840 (B)
Catholic University of America, Washington, D.C. 20064 (B)
Clarke College, Dubuque, Iowa 52001 (B)
College Misericordia, Dallas, Pa. 18612 (B)
College of Mt. St. Joseph on the Ohio, Mt. St. Joseph, Ohio 45051 (B)
College of St. Teresa, Winona, Minn. 55987 (B)
Colorado State University, Fort Collins, Colo. 80523 (B)
De Paul University, Chicago, Ill. 60614 (B)
Duquesne University, Pittsburgh, Pa. 15219 (B)
East Carolina University, Greenville, N.C. 27834 (B)
Eastern New Mexico University, Portales, N. Mex. 88130 (B)
Elizabethtown College, Elizabethtown, Pa. 17022 (B)
Florida State University, Tallahassee, Fla. 32306 (B, M)
Georgia College, Milledgeville, Ga. 31061 (B)

Henderson State University, Arkadelphia, Ark. 71923 (B)
Illinois State University, Normal, Ill. 61761 (B)
Indiana University at Fort Wayne, Fort Wayne, Ind. 46805 (B)
Loyola University, New Orleans, La. 70118 (B, M)
Maryville College, St. Louis, Mo. 63141 (B)
Michigan State University, East Lansing, Mich. 48824 (B, M)
Montclair State College, Upper Montclair, N.J. 07043 (B)
Ohio University, Athens, Ohio 45701 (B)
Phillips University, Enid, Okla. 73701 (B)
Queens College, Charlotte, N.C. 28274 (B)
Slippery Rock State College, Slippery Rock, Pa. 16057 (B)
Southern Methodist University, Dallas, Tex. 75275 (B, M)
State University College at Fredonia, Fredonia, N.Y. 14063 (B)
State University College at New Paltz, New Paltz, N.Y. 12561 (B)
Texas Woman's University, Denton, Tex. 76204 (B, M)
University of Dayton, Dayton, Ohio 45469 (B)
University of Evansville, Evansville, Ind. 47702 (B)
University of Georgia, Athens, Ga. 30602 (B, M)
University of Iowa, Iowa City, Iowa 52242 (B)
University of Kansas, Lawrence, Kans. 66045 (B, M)
University of Miami, Coral Gables, Fla. 33124 (B, M)

University of Minnesota, Minneapolis, Minn. 55455
(B)
University of Missouri at Kansas City, Kansas City,
Mo. 64111 (B)
University of the Pacific, Stockton, Calif. 95211
(B)
University of Wisconsin at Eau Claire, Eau Claire,
Wis. 54701 (B)
University of Wisconsin at Milwaukee, Milwaukee,
Wis. 53201 (B)
University of Wisconsin at Oshkosh, Oshkosh, Wis.
54901 (B)
Wartburg College, Waverly, Iowa 50677 (B)
Wayne State University, Detroit, Mich. 48202 (B)
West Texas State University, Canyon, Tex. 79016
(B)
Western Illinois University, Macomb, Ill. 61455
(B)
Western Michigan University, Kalamazoo, Mich.
49001 (B, M)
Willamette University, Salem, Oreg. 97301 (B)
William Carey College, Hattiesburg, Miss. 39401
(B)

If you would like additional information about careers in music therapy, write to the National Association for Music Therapy, Inc., P. O. Box 610, Lawrence, Kans. 66044.

In addition to these three major creative-arts therapies, there are such truly aborning therapies as *poetry therapy* and *puppet therapy.*

Poetry therapists use poetry as the tool by which to

bring about desirable changes in the mode of behavior of persons with emotional and mental problems. By means of poetry, patients are able to bring forth emotions and thoughts, at times even self-destructive ones, that lie deep within them. The poetry therapists, guided by the patients' poetic expressions, may present their recommendations to the other members of the therapeutic team.

Puppet therapists use puppetry as the therapeutic tool. This tool is especially helpful with hospitalized children. These children project their feelings, particularly their aggressions and hostilities, onto the puppets which serve as safe outlets for the children's negative emotions. In this manner of play, children may act out their home or other life situations. The information which the puppet therapists gain thereby is used to improve the total treatment process.

Poetry therapy and puppet therapy are so very young that career opportunities in these fields are very limited. Isolated courses related to these fields are offered in some colleges and universities throughout the country, but there are as yet no formal degree programs. If you find poetry therapy or puppet therapy attractive, have creative talent in either of these areas, and have obtained a bachelor's degree with a major in psychology, you would do well to visit the hospitals in your city and suggest the addition of these tools to their therapeutic programs.

All creative-arts therapists should, of course, be talented in their respective branch of creative arts. They should like to work with ill people and be genuinely interested in helping them. Emotional stability, patience and tact are essential. The work of these therapists can often be frustrating, for progress of ill people is often slow; these therapists must, therefore, have the ability to withstand this frustration. Every bit of progress, however, brings tremendous gratification to these therapists.

The number of creative-arts therapists is small. With the passage of time, more creative-arts therapists will be added to the staffs of hospitals and other institutions. The growth potential of career opportunities in these fields is very good.

9

Flowers That Bloom in the Spring— and Winter, Summer and Fall

Flowers—and even plants that do not flower—generally have an uplifting effect on people. Plants and flowers are among the most psychologically beneficial gifts.

Is a friend or relative in the hospital, ill at home, feeling depressed, having a birthday, or involved in some other occurrence or occasion? If you send that person flowers or a plant, you will thereby, in all probability, make that person happier.

Flowers are assembled and arranged in a manner befitting the purpose for which they are being purchased and the person to whom they are being sent. *Floral designers* are the people who do this assembling and arranging. They first determine the reasons for the flowers and then proceed to express the sentiments of the sender. They may choose natural or artificial flowers and foliage. Then they fashion and design the floral pieces and decorations.

The floral designers wire, pin, and wrap the stems with special floral tape. They thus assemble bouquets, corsages, centerpieces, wreaths, and miscellaneous other floral designs as the occasion or purpose may warrant.

They plan and design varied floral settings for special events, such as balls, conventions, parties, and weddings. They also decorate buildings, such as churches, temples, and private homes, for special occasions.

These designers must possess a knowledge of flower forms and shapes, plant materials, and floral design. They must know how to assemble decorative potted plants in addition to flowers. Often they are called upon to prepare floral arrangements for funerals and this calls for a special understanding and creativity.

Floral designers must be knowledgeable about the seasonal availability of varied plants and flowers. They must be familiar with the growth characteristics of potted plants as well as the names and lasting qualities of many different flowers.

Sometimes, customers may specify the flowers and designs they desire. Often, however, they leave this to the discretion of the designer and only stipulate the purpose of the flowers and/or plants. The designers prepare a written order in which they indicate the customer's preference, if any, or the designer's suggestion, as to color and type of flower or plant, cost and time, date and place to which the plant or floral arrangement will be delivered.

Those who would like to become floral designers are generally trained on the job by an experienced floral designer or by the manager of a retail flower shop. However, an increasing number of young people who aspire to such careers are taking courses in floral arrangements in public and private schools and junior colleges. Some take special programs in floriculture including courses in flower marketing and retail-flower-shop management. On-the-job training, ranging from several months to one or two years, is essential even after the formal training.

Beginners generally assemble simple arrangements involving one type of flower. As they become more skilled at this form of designing, they advance to more complex arrangements, involving flowers of different shapes and colors.

Designing talent and creative ability are essential in this career, as well as a knowledge of flowers. Manual dexterity and keen color vision are needed in order to be capable of arranging flowers of varied colors, shapes, and sizes in attractive patterns.

There were about thirty-five thousand floral designers at work throughout the United States in 1977. Almost all of them worked in retail flower shops, found just about everywhere in large and small cities and towns throughout the nation. Many floral designers own and manage their own flower shops.

It is anticipated that sales of flowers will increase significantly as time goes on. People enjoy buying flowers and plants for themselves and as gifts for others. The employment outlook for floral designers is, therefore, expected to be good and to increase faster than the average for all occupations through the 1980s.

If you would like to obtain further information about careers in floral design, write to the Society of American Florists and Ornamental Horticulturists, 901 N. Washington St., Alexandria, Va. 22314.

Horticulture is the science of the cultivation of orchards and garden plants; this involves flowers, fruits, vegetables and/or ornamental plants.

Horticulturists aim to improve plant-culture methods in order to increase crop quality and yields and also to beautify communities, homes, parks, and other places. The *ornamental horticulturists* are concerned with ornamental plants, such as aquatic plants, flowering bulbs, cacti, herbaceous annuals and perennials, vines, woody flower-bearing shrubs and trees, and other shrubs and trees.

Ornamental horticulturists who specialize in flower culture are called *floriculturists*. Those who specialize in the culture and artistic planting and trimming of trees are known as *arboriculturists*.

Ornamental horticulture, which includes floriculture and arboriculture, has recently brought about the birth of another unusual career. This career is so new that its titles are many and varied. Many new luxury apartment houses and office buildings have arisen in recent years in large cities, and even in smaller cities, throughout the land. These residential and office buildings have spacious lobbies and some have large outdoor areas surrounding the buildings. In these lobbies and areas many have huge potted plants, small trees and shrubs, and varied floral arrangements. The persons who tend to these plants and flowers are known by ever so many titles, including *building horticulturist, horticultural engineer,* and *plants engineer.*

This career is so very, very young that there are no specified qualifications for entry into it. Young people who have received academic training in ornamental horticulture and who would be interested in such positions should apply directly to the building managers. If these young people, while they are still attending school, see new buildings being built in their city, they should apply for these positions at this early stage; when they complete their studies in ornamental horticulture, the buildings may be up and the positions may be waiting for them.

Another new career in the field of horticulture is that of the *horticultural therapist*. Horticultural therapists work in hospitals and nursing homes where they try to help patients become more interested in their surroundings. These therapists combine a knowledge of psychological techniques with a knowledge of plants, flowers, and gardening. Patients are helped to express themselves by means of small garden plots. This therapy helps the patients to work together; it increases socialization and reduces feelings of isolation.

The number of horticultural therapists is still very small and requirements for entry into this career have not been formulated. Those who would like to become horticultural therapists should include the basic psychology courses and ornamental horticulture courses in their college studies.

Following are the names and addresses of institutions of higher education that offer two- and four-year programs in *ornamental horticulture,* leading to the associate's and bachelor's degrees, respectively, with the A and B indicating the specific degree program(s) offered:

Auburn University, Auburn, Ala. 36830 (B)
Baldwin (Abraham) Agricultural College, Tifton, Ga. 31794 (A)
Becker Junior College, Leicester, Mass. 01524 (A)
Brigham Young University, Provo, Utah 84602 (B)

Broward Community College, Fort Lauderdale, Fla. 33301 (A)
Butte College, Oroville, Calif. 95965 (A)
California Polytechnic State University, San Luis Obispo, Calif. 93407 (B)
California State Polytechnic University, Pomona, Calif. 91768 (B)
California State University, Fresno, Calif. 93740 (B)
Chabet College, Hayward, Calif. 94545 (A)
Clackamas Community College, Oregon City, Oreg. 97045 (A)
Clark Technical College, Springfield, Ohio 45501 (A)
Clemson University, Clemson, S.C. 29631 (B)
College of DuPage, Glen Ellyn, Ill. 60137 (A)
College of Lake County, Grayslake, Ill. 60030 (A)
College of the Canyons, Valencia, Calif. 91355 (A)
College of the Redwoods, Eureka, Calif. 95501 (A)
Colorado State University, Fort Collins, Colo. 80523 (B)
Community College of Denver, North Campus, Denver, Colo. 80020 (A)
Community College of the Finger Lakes, Canandaigua, N.Y. 14424 (A)
Cook College (Rutgers University), New Brunswick, N.J. 08903 (B)
Cornell University, Ithaca, N.Y. 14853 (B)
Daytona Beach Community College, Daytona Beach, Fla. 32015 (A)
Delaware Valley College of Sciences & Agriculture, Doylestown, Pa. 18901 (B)

Eastern Kentucky University, Richmond, Ky. 40475 (A, B)

Eastern Nazarene College, Quincy, Mass. 02170 (A)

Edmonds Community College, Lynnwood, Wash. 98036 (A)

Elgin Community College, Elgin, Ill. 60120 (A)

Fayetteville Technical Institute, Fayetteville, N.C. 28303 (A)

Ferris State College, Big Rapids, Mich. 49307 (A)

Florida Agricultural and Mechanical University, Tallahassee, Fla. 32307 (A, B)

Forsyth Technical Institute, Winston-Salem, N.C. 27103 (A)

Glenville State College, Glenville, W. Va. 26351 (A)

Hancock (Allan) College, Santa Maria, Calif. 93454 (A)

Iowa State University of Science and Technology, Ames, Iowa 50011 (B)

Joliet Junior College, Joliet, Ill. 60436 (A)

Kansas State University, Manhattan, Kans. 66506 (A)

Kirkwood Community College, Cedar Rapids, Iowa 52406 (A)

Lake City Community College, Lake City, Fla. 32055 (A)

McHenry County College, Crystal Lake, Ill. 60014 (A)

Mercer County Community College, Trenton, N.J. 08690 (A)

Metropolitan Technical Community College, Omaha, Nebr. 68137 (A)

Mississippi State University, State College, Miss. 39762 (B)

Monterey Peninsula College, Monterey, Calif. 93940 (A)

Moorpark College, Moorpark, Calif. 93021 (A)

Morehead State University, Morehead, Ky. 40351 (A, B)

Mount Hood Community College, Gresham, Oreg. 97030 (A)

Mount San Antonio College, Walnut, Calif. 91789 (A)

New Mexico State University, Las Cruces, N. Mex. 88003 (B)

Nicholls State University, Thibodaux, La. 70301 (A)

North Dakota State University, Fargo, N. Dak. 58102 (A, B)

North Iowa Area Community College, Mason City, Iowa 50401 (A)

Northeast Louisiana University, Monroe, La. 71203 (A)

Ohio State University Agricultural Technical Institute, Wooster, Ohio 44691 (A)

Orange Coast College, Costa Mesa, Calif. 92626 (A)

Polk Community College, Winter Haven, Fla. 33880 (A)

Purdue University, West Lafayette, Ind. 47907 (A, B)

Richland College, Dallas, Tex. 75243 (A)

Ricks College, Rexburg, Idaho 83440 (A)

Saddleback Community College, Mission Valley, Calif. 92675 (A)

St. Louis Community College at Meramec, Kirkwood, Mo. 63122 (A)

Santa Barbara City College, Santa Barbara, Calif. 93109 (A)

Santa Rosa Junior College, Santa Rosa, Calif. 95401 (A)

Sierra College, Rocklin, Calif. 95677 (A)

Southern Illinois University, Carbondale, Ill. 62901 (B)

Southwestern College, Winfield, Kans. 67156 (B)

State University of New York Agricultural & Technical College, Alfred, N.Y. 14802 (A)

State University of New York Agricultural & Technical College, Cobleskill, N.Y. 12043 (A)

State University of New York Agricultural & Technical College, Farmingdale, N.Y. 11735 (A)

State University of New York Agricultural & Technical College, Morrisville, N.Y. 13408 (A)

Surry Community College, Dobson, N.C. 27017 (A)

Temple University, Philadelphia, Pa. 19122 (A)

Texas A & M University, College Station, Tex. 77843 (B)

Texas State Technical Institute, Waco, Tex. 76705 (A)

Texas Tech University, Lubbock, Tex. 79409 (B)

Trident Technical College, Charleston, S.C. 29411 (A)

Triton College, River Grove, Ill. 60171 (A)

University of Florida, Gainesville, Fla. 32611 (B)

University of Georgia, Athens, Ga. 30602 (B)

University of Idaho, Moscow, Idaho 83843 (B)

University of Illinois at Urbana-Champaign, Urbana, Ill. 61801 (B)

University of Maryland, College Park, Md. 20742 (B)

University of Massachusetts, Amherst, Mass. 01003 (A)

University of Minnesota Technical College, Crookston, Minn. 56716 (A)

University of Minnesota Technical College, Waseca, Minn. 56093 (A)

University of Southern Louisiana, Lafayette, La. 70504 (A)

University of Tennessee, Knoxville, Tenn. 37916 (B)

Vincennes University, Vincennes, Ind. 47591 (A)

Western Kentucky University, Bowling Green, Ky. 42101 (B)

Wilkes Community College, Wilkesboro, N.C. 28697 (A)

Yavapai College, Prescott, Ariz. 86301 (A)

For additional information about careers in horticulture, write to the American Horticultural Society, Mount Vernon, Va. 22121.

10

Careers from Insects, Harmful and Beneficial

There are all kinds of insects, beneficial as well as harmful. *Entomologists* are the scientists who study both types of insects. Essentially, they are agricultural scientists who perform research and other studies on insects and their relations to plant and animal life.

Entomologists direct their research toward discovering methods by which harmful pests may be eliminated and beneficial insects aided in the roles they play in the elimination of the pests. They identify and plot the distribution of these harmful insects that do damage to humans, animals, growing crops, and agricultural commodities during their shipment, storage, processing, and distribution.

Among the pests that the entomologists aim to control and eliminate are such harmful insects as fruit flies, gypsy and brown-tail moths, Japanese beetles, and forest insects. Entomologists help to develop new and improved insecticides to destroy these pests. They also develop ways of encouraging the growth and spread of beneficial insects, such as bees and those which are used as foods by birds and fish.

126

Some entomologists specialize in the study of one particular insect. Thus, some become *sericulturists* and specialize in silkworm culture and breeding. A larger group consists of the *apiculturists;* they specialize in the study of bee culture and breeding.

Apiculturists strive to improve bee strains by using selective breeding. They conduct experiments on the causes and control of bee diseases. They study varied factors which affect the yields of nectar and pollen on plants used by bees, and do research on the phases of pollination. They also conduct tests to determine the vitamin and other content of miscellaneous honeys.

Entomologists are employed by federal, state, county, and municipal government agencies. They also work for colleges and universities, agricultural experiment stations, and varied companies in the vast field of agribusiness. The demand for entomologists exceeds the supply and the employment outlook in this profession is, therefore, very favorable.

The bachelor's degree with a major in biology, and specifically entomology, is needed for entry positions in this career. The master's degree and, increasingly, the doctorate, are becoming necessary for advancement.

Following are the names and addresses of institutions of higher education that offer bachelor's, master's, and doctor's degree programs in *entomology,* with the B, M, and D indicating the specific degree program(s) offered:

Arizona State University, Tempe, Ariz. 85281 (B)
Auburn University, Auburn, Ala. 36830 (B, M, D)

Bowling Green State University, Bowling Green, Ohio 43403 (B)

Brigham Young University, Provo, Utah 84602 (B M, D)

California State College at Stanislaus, Turlock, Calif. 95380 (B)

California State University, Fresno, Calif. 93740 (B)

Clemson University, Clemson, S.C. 29631 (B, M, D)

Colorado State University, Fort Collins, Colo. 80523 (B, M, D)

Cook College (Rutgers University), New Brunswick, N.J. 08903 (B)

Cornell University, Ithaca, N.Y. 14853 (B, M, D)

Fordham University, Bronx, N.Y. 10458 (D)

Iowa State University of Science and Technology, Ames, Iowa 50011 (B, M, D)

Kansas State University, Manhattan, Kans. 66506 (B, M)

Kent State University, Kent, Ohio 44242 (M)

Louisiana State University and Agricultural and Mechanical College, Baton Rouge, La. 70803 (B, M, D)

Marlboro College, Marlboro, Vt. 05344 (B)

Michigan State University, East Lansing, Mich. 48824 (B, M, D)

Montana State University, Bozeman, Mont. 59715 (M, D)

Nebraska Wesleyan University, Lincoln, Nebr. 68504 (B)

New Mexico State University, Las Cruces, N. Mex. 88003 (B)

North Carolina State University, Raleigh, N.C. 27607 (B, M, D)

North Dakota State University, Fargo, N. Dak. 58102 (B, M, D)

Northwestern University, Evanston, Ill. 60201 (M, D)

Ohio State University, Columbus, Ohio 43210 (B, M, D)

Ohio University, Athens, Ohio 45701 (M, D)

Oregon State University, Corvallis, Oreg. 97331 (B, M, D)

Pennsylvania State University, University Park, Pa. 16802 (B, M, D)

Purdue University, West Lafayette, Ind. 47907 (B, M, D)

San Jose State University, San Jose, Calif. 95192 (B)

South Dakota State University, Brookings, S. Dak. 57006 (B, M)

State University of New York College of Environmental Science and Forestry, Syracuse, N.Y. 13210 (B, M)

Texas A & M University, College Station, Tex. 77843 (B, M, D)

Texas Tech University, Lubbock, Tex. 79409 (B, M)

Tufts University, Medford, Mass. 02155 (B)

University of Alabama, University, Ala. 35486 (B, M, D)

University of Arizona, Tucson, Ariz. 85721 (B, M, D)

University of Arkansas, Fayetteville, Ark. 72701
(B, M, D)
University of California, Berkeley, Calif. 94720 (B,
M, D)
University of California, Davis, Calif. 95616 (B,
M, D)
University of California, Riverside, Calif. 92521 (B,
M)
University of Delaware, Newark, Del. 19711 (B, M,
D)
University of Florida, Gainesville, Fla. 32611 (B,
M, D)
University of Hawaii at Manoa, Honolulu, Hawaii
96822 (B, M, D)
University of Idaho, Moscow, Idaho 83843 (B, M,
D)
University of Illinois at Urbana-Champaign, Urbana,
Ill. 61801 (B, M, D)
University of Kentucky, Lexington, Ky. 40506 (B,
M, D)
University of Maryland, College Park, Md. 20742
(B, M, D)
University of Massachusetts, Amherst, Mass. 01003
(B, M, D)
University of Minnesota, Twin Cities, Minneapolis,
Minn. 55455 (B, M, D)
University of Missouri, Columbia, Mo. 65201 (M,
D)
University of Nebraska, Lincoln, Nebr. 68588 (B,
M, D)
University of New Hampshire, Durham, N.H. 03824
(B, M)

University of Pittsburgh, Johnstown, Pa. 15904 (B)
University of Wisconsin, Madison, Wis. 53706 (B, M, D)
University of Wyoming, Laramie, Wyo. 82071 (B, M, D)
Virginia Polytechnic Institute and State University, Blacksburg, Va. 34061 (M, D)
Washington State University, Pullman, Wash. 99163 (B, M, D)

If you would like further information about the career of the entomologist and/or the apiculturist, write to the U.S. Department of Agriculture, Washington, D.C. 20250.

Allied to the apiculturists are the *apiarists,* otherwise known as *beekeepers.* They are also called *bee farmers, bee raisers,* and *honey producers.*

Beekeepers assemble beehives and cultivate bees for the production of honey and the pollination of crops. They prepare honeycomb frames and insert the honeycombs of bees into beehives. The hives are specially created wooden boxes that facilitate the growth of the colonies of bees. The beekeepers extract the honey, bottle it, and arrange with purchasers for the sale of this honey. They also collect royal jelly from queen-bee cells and sell this jelly as a base for cosmetics and as health food.

In addition to the commercial beekeepers, there are those who raise bees as a hobby and others who indulge in beekeeping as a part-time venture. The commercial beekeepers generally maintain at least two hundred colonies of bees. Beekeepers must like to work outdoors, be knowledgeable about agricultural science, and have keen senses of hearing, sight, smell, and taste.

It is advisable that young people who are interested in a career in beekeeping start their beekeeping activities as a hobby or gain experience by working during summer vacations for a commercial beekeeper.

Courses in apiculture are included in many college entomology departments. The beekeeper who obtains a bachelor's degree with major concentration in entomology could combine beekeeping activities with a career in entomology. Check the preceding section on the career of the entomologist for the names and addresses of institutions of higher education offering bachelor's degree programs in entomology.

You may obtain government pamphlets on beekeeping from the U.S. Department of Agriculture, Washington, D.C. 20250. For additional information on beekeeping, write to the Bee Industries Association of America, Hamilton, Ill. 62341.

Even some of the best of homes are pest-infested. These "pests" include mice and rats as well as such common household insects as ants, flies, roaches, silverfish, and termites. Termites do damage to property and eat away at private homes. The other pests contaminate food and spread disease. *Pest controllers* aim to protect our health and property by destroying these pests.

Pest controllers spray chemical solutions or toxic gases to kill pests of all sorts. They may place poisonous pastes, bait, or mechanical traps in rooms and other areas that harbor pests. They may fumigate rooms and buildings using special sprays.

Pest controllers may be *termite specialists* or *pest-control route workers*. Some pest controllers serve in both capacities. One effective treatment often keeps a building free of termites for several years. Termite specialists, therefore, may work one or more days in a particular building and then not need to return to that building for a long time. This contrasts with the work of the pest-control route workers. The latter must return frequently to the homes in which they work because the pests they strive to destroy are difficult to eradicate.

Pest-control route workers aim to exterminate common household insects and rodents from such places as apartment houses, private homes, hotels, food stores, restaurants, and other structures where these pests may nest. They generally work alone, in contrast to the termite specialists, who often work in pairs or have helpers to assist them. In one day, route workers may cover a dozen or more places and may revisit many of them a week to a month later.

Pest controllers must have a good knowledge of chemical pesticides to enable them to select the safest and most effective pesticide for each individual extermination assignment. They must be aware of the living habits and hiding places of the different insects and rodents. Great care must be taken in properly placing poisonous baits to be sure that there is no danger to children and pets.

There are no specific educational requirements for entry into the field of pest control. Preference is given to high school graduates for positions as *pest-control trainees*. High school courses in chemistry are desirable. Since pest controllers must explain and "sell" their services to their customers, courses in sales and business arithmetic are of value too. Some community colleges have begun to offer two-year programs in pest control. Graduates of such programs generally do not need to go through the "trainee" stage. Pest controllers must be licensed by the state in which they work.

Those who would like careers as pest controllers should first determine whether or not they are allergic to the chemicals in the various pesticides. Working conditions in this field are far from ideal but many enjoy the challenges. There are also opportunities for self-employment here.

There were approximately twenty-eight thousand pest controllers at work in the United States in 1977. The control of pests seems to be a never-ending problem. This is, in great measure, due to urban congestion, deterioration of many buildings, and the fact that pests reproduce rapidly and often become resistant to certain pesticides. The employment outlook in this field, therefore, appears very favorable for the 1980s.

If you would like additional information about the career of the pest controller, write to the National Pest Control Association, Inc., 8150 Leesburg Pike, Vienna, Va. 22180.

11
A Potpourri of Unique Opportunity

There are a number of careers that are so unique you may not have heard of them, although they could not be classed as new, for they have been in existence for many years. There are other careers that may not appear to be very unique, but they are very new. Because of the nature and/or newness of these careers, little has been written and little is generally known about them.

Have you ever heard of *topiarists?* Topiary is the art of clipping and trimming miscellaneous plants, hedges, flowers, or entire gardens into unusual shapes. The topiarists are the experts in the art and practice of topiary. They cut, trim, and train plants to form unusual designs.

Professional topiarists are capable of forming a multitude of dfferent topiary shapes. They may form the initials or names of the homeowners for whom they are doing this artistry or they may make the figures and shapes of animals, characters from the comic strips, caricatures, religious symbols, and ever so many other designs that they have been commissioned to produce.

Some topiarists use what they call the free-form pruning method. With a pair of pruning shears, they cut and trim shrubs and hedges to form a desired pattern. They work without any artificial frames around which the plants must grow. This permits the topiarists to easily alter any design if such alteration is desired.

Other topiarists work with wire frames. They place these frames over the plants or hedges and permit them to grow into the frames, thus forming the desired designs and shapes. When the plant grows and extends above and beyond the frames, it is pruned back to the frame-form.

All homeowners who prune their hedges into round shapes, square shapes or step designs are amateur topiarists. Although this is an old and highly regarded profession in Europe, it is estimated that there are probably less than one hundred professional topiarists in the United States. This career calls for a knowledge of art, gardening, landscape design, and horticulture. The topiarists must carefully select the plants that are appropriate for the climate and soil of the garden in which they are working and for the design they hope to create. Some topiarists have their own greenhouses in which they cultivate their own plants and flowers.

Professional topiarists must have creative ability and artistic talent. They need training in horticulture and landscape design, plus a sense of color, form, and perspective. Frequently, topiarists form geometric patterns, such as circular, rectangular, or hexagonal or octagonal shapes. A knowledge of geometry and the ability to chart dimensions are of importance to topiarists. Sometimes topiarists are commissioned to produce giant-size figures, such as are sometimes seen in large parks, amusement centers, and botanical gardens; those who do this must have no fear of heights.

There are no formal training programs to prepare a

person for a career in topiary. Those who are interested in such a career should consider the programs in ornamental horticulture listed in Chapter 7, and also include courses in art and landscape design in their academic programs. On-the-job training from a professional topiarist is very important for beginners in this field. High school and college students could get valuable experience as helpers doing odd jobs for gardeners during their summer vacations.

For further information about a career in topiary, write to the American Horticultural Society, Mount Vernon, Va. 22121.

When you hear the title *"space analyst,"* you probably think of someone in the field of aerospace, don't you? Well, if this is what you think, you are wrong. The "space" involved here is "inner" not "outer" space—more specifically, office space.

Space analysts are also known as *office designers.* They plan office layouts. This planning is not done simply to give an office a beautiful appearance. Essentially, its purpose is to increase the efficiency of employee work production by facilitating work flow from one area to another and by making the employees more comfortable. Improved efficiency results in increased profits and this is the goal of the employers.

In planning the layout of an office, the space analyst starts by meeting with the office administrators. The latter explain the nature of the office setup, the specific work activities of the employees, and how the nature of each employee's work interrelates with that of the other employees. The number of employees on the floor or section of a floor and the size and dimensions of the total work area are taken into consideration. The purpose behind the office activities is an important factor in the successful planning of the office's layout. The layout of the offices of a manufacturing plant, for example, will differ from that of the offices in a publishing house or advertising agency.

The space analyst meets with the office employees and elicits from them their individual desires and needs. From these employees, the analyst also determines the objectives they would like the office layout to meet. The space analyst then adds this information to that which was gathered from the office administrators, analyzes this information, and proceeds to draw up an initial layout program. This program reflects the objectives of the office and integrates space limitations and physical conditions. If this program is approved, the space analyst then prepares a graphic design of the proposed office layout.

Space analysts arrange for furniture to be moved, existing walls to be torn down, and partitions to be erected. Some offices have an "open plan." This means there are low partitions and few, if any, walls, so that work can pass easily from one desk to another. Other offices have a layout called a "closed plan." Here the office personnel have walled-in, closed-door offices to enable individual employees to work in private, quiet surroundings.

Office design and space planning call for a knowledge of architecture, interior design, art, and psychology. There are no specific curricula in office design in any of the colleges or universities. Since office design essentially combines architecture and interior design, the best means of preparing for a career as a space analyst would be to attend a school of architecture and include courses in interior design and basic psychology in the program of studies, or to attend a school of interior design and include courses in architecture, building design, and basic psychology.

Some colleges are beginning to add courses in industrial-space planning to their curricula. These stress the importance of an understanding of human needs, since space analysts play an important role in improving the surroundings and thereby the morale of office personnel, which, in turn, increases employee productivity.

Space analysts must have designing ability, artistic talent, and the ability to express themselves verbally and graphically. Those who work for large design firms generally work as members of a team. Others may work alone as free-lance office designers. In 1977, there were about twenty-two thousand space analysts at work throughout the country. Future employment opportunities will depend upon how much new office construction will take place; it is anticipated that the situation will be favorable throughout the 1980s.

If you would like additional information about the career of the space analyst–office designer, it is advisable that you write to both of the following: American Institute of Architecture, 1735 New York Ave., Washington, D.C. 20036, and the American Society of Interior Design, 730 Fifth Ave., New York, N.Y. 10019.

Vending machines may be found just about everywhere. The vending-machine business is one of our major industries today. It is a young industry whose rapid growth began after World War II.

The range of items that can be purchased from vending machines appears to be almost endless. These machines offer everything from a package of chewing gum to a full-course hot meal, from a package of cigarettes to items of clothing, and from a toothbrush to a vast array of items, necessary, luxury, and otherwise.

These machines must be kept in properly functioning condition. *Vending-machine repairers* are the people who maintain these machines in good working order. These repairers transport these machines to the locations at which they are to be placed, inspect the sites to see that all is well, and then proceed to install the machines. They assemble new vending machines according to instructions and make the necessary water, electricity, and drain connections. They test the operation of these machines and correct any malfunctions.

Vending-machine repairers repair the machines at the vending locations whenever possible. If major repairs are required, they take the machines or components to the shop. Vandalism, abuse from purchasers, and general wear and tear from everyday use make frequent repair of these machines necessary. These repairers remove dents from the cabinets, install new panels, and weld broken brackets, using welding equipment where needed.

An important part of the vending-machine repairer's job is what is known as "preventive maintenance." This is the attempt to prevent repair problems before they start. The repairers, therefore, clean and lubricate the machine parts periodically. They clean the electrical contact points and see to it that there are no loose electrical wires. If they find faulty parts, they replace them immediately. They also test the coin and change-making mechanisms to prevent any malfunctions.

Many vending-machine repairers also stock these machines with merchandise. Those who do this are known, too, as *vending-machine repairers–route workers*. Those who work with food-vending machines must be acquainted with the state public health and sanitation standards; they must also know the standards as established under local plumbing codes.

If the machines are dispensing hot or cold food items, the repairers use thermometers and pressure gauges to test the heating and refrigeration systems. They also use measuring cups to test whether the proper proportions and amounts of products or ingredients are being delivered. The repairer–route workers not only keep the machines well supplied, but also collect money and fill the coin and currency changers. They also maintain daily records of the merchandise they distribute to these machines.

There were approximately 5 million vending machines of all sorts throughout the United States in 1977, and about twenty-five thousand repairers worked at maintaining them. Most of these repairers were employed by vending service companies that install vending machines and then maintain, repair and stock them. Some are self-employed as independent operators of one or more vending machines.

Beginners enter this career as *general shop helpers,* working on machines that have been returned to the shop for major repair work, or as *vending-machine route drivers,* who only stock the machines and do no repair work. Among these beginners, those who have mechanical aptitude may be appointed to the position of *vending-machine-repairer trainee.* Graduates of vocational high schools who have completed courses in machine repair, electricity, and refrigeration may be appointed directly to trainee positions.

Vending-machine repairers learn their trade essentially

via on-the-job training. This training may range from six months to two years in length, depending upon the trainees' previous formal education and their mechanical skills. As time goes on, vending machines are becoming more and more complex and employers are encouraging their repairers to take evening courses in advanced machine operation and repair. Additionally, some technical and community colleges are adding two-year programs in automatic-vending-machine technology to their curricula.

The vending machine industry is expanding with the increase in our nation's population. Employment opportunities for repairers and independent operators will grow with the nation's growth. However, it must be remembered that this is a small occupation.

For further information about a career as a vending-machine repairer, contact the National Automatic Merchandising Association, 7 S. Dearborn St., Chicago, Ill. 60603. Information about schools offering training programs in automatic-vending-machine technology may be obtained from the National Association of Trade and Technical Schools, 2021 L St. N.W., Washington, D.C. 20036.

How many records did you buy last year? What prompted you to buy the ones you did? Although you may not have been aware of it, it was probably the record-album cover that attracted you to one record rather than to another.

The record industry is a $1.5 billion industry. The design and art work on the album covers are important factors in the sale of the records. Even big-name performers, whose names are quite sufficient to bring about huge sales, are demanding top-grade artistry on their album covers. Some art work on album covers is designed to provoke controversy. Others have a "come-hither" attraction. The covers of classical records tend toward a more conservative form of art work.

Record-album designers must have creative talent and artistic ability. They may be employed by record producing companies or work for advertising agencies that handle the accounts of record companies. There are also designers who have their own independent studios; after establishing a reputation for designing unusually attractive album covers, they are able to obtain their own freelance assignments.

The routes to employment as a record-album designer are many. The would-be designer may go to a four-year college and major in art, or complete a specialized curriculum in design at a two-year community college, or attend a special school of art and design. Although the training is important, insofar as obtaining employment, it is of lesser importance than the candidate's innate artistic talent.

Sales of records are soaring and it is anticipated that they will continue to do so. Attractive album-cover graphics are in great demand, but the field is highly competitive.

A "Grammy" award is given annually for the best art work on a record-album cover. This award is given by the National Academy of Recording Arts and Sciences. If you would like additional information, write to the National Academy of Recording Arts and Sciences, 21 West 58th Street, New York, N.Y. 10019.

Some people with artistic talent direct their creativity into the channels of another unique art career, namely that of the *courtroom sketcher*. This is more a part-time, rather than a full-time, career, but there are those artists who find the excitement of the courtroom a stimulating setting for their art activities. Photographers are not allowed inside courtrooms.

Those who seek to become courtroom sketchers generally start by attending trials and sketching the participants on their own. They gather together into a portfolio their best sketches. Then, they visit the art directors of newspapers, magazines, and television stations, and show them their samples. If the art directors are impressed with their work, they will contact them as assignments arise.

In view of the nature of courtroom activity, a courtroom sketcher may sketch the participants in one trial that lasts for only a few days, in another that extends for a few weeks, and, in a rare case, of a few months' duration. Since these are not full-time positions, courtroom sketchers often also accept other art work assignments, such as doing varied illustrations for books, magazines, and newspapers.

Like the record-album designers, the courtroom sketchers may acquire their art training in special art institutes or in the art curricula of two-year or four-year colleges, but the major factor is the possession of artistic talent. The courtroom sketchers need good eyesight, a keen sense of accuracy, and the ability to sketch quickly the particularly newsworthy people and happenings in the courtroom. These are limited, but gratifying, careers.

For the names and addresses of schools offering special training programs in art applicable to the careers of the record-album designer and the courtroom sketcher, write to the National Art Education Association, 1916 Association Drive, Reston, Va. 22091.

The mopeds are here—and their sales are booming and zooming. What is a moped? It is a motorized bicycle, or a hybrid of a motorcycle and a bicycle. Its name is derived from the two words, "motor" and "pedal."

Mopeds have long been popular in Europe. In France alone, there are at least 6 million mopeds in use. The accident rate is much lower than the rate for motorcycles and even less than the rate for automobiles. In the United States, mopeds were relatively unknown before the oil crisis of 1974. In 1975, approximately twenty-five thousand mopeds were sold throughout the United States; in 1976, this figure rose to about seventy-five thousand. In 1977, sales zoomed to approximately two hundred thousand. It is anticipated that as time goes on, the sale of mopeds will continue to rise.

Mopeds have one-cylinder engines that are capable of getting anywhere from 120 to 200 miles per gallon of gasoline. Mopeds have handlebar brakes. When the motor is disconnected, they can be driven by the pedals. In view of gasoline shortages and the high cost of gasoline, mopeds have become a popular alternative means of transportation.

Many states have enacted moped legislation regulating the use of mopeds. Laws have been passed stipulating the minimum age of drivers and the kinds of licenses, if any, that are required. If you would like to obtain information about state laws regulating mopeds, write to the Mortorized Bicycle Association, 1001 Connecticut Ave. N.W., Washington, D.C. 20036.

In addition to the matter of legislation, there are many valuable suggestions that are offered to moped drivers when they purchase these vehicles. It is advisable that these drivers have annual tune-ups of their vehicles and maintain them in good working condition; these drivers should be aware of the limitations and capabilities of their vehicles. All moped drivers are urged to wear protective headgear, preferably a brightly colored motorcycle helmet. Since the moped may not be visible to automobile drivers, moped drivers should place reflective lights and tall, bright-orange bicycle flags on their vehicles. Above all, moped enthusiasts should receive basic operating instructions from the dealers from whom they have purchased their vehicles and become skilled in the operation of these vehicles before they drive in any heavily trafficked areas.

Interestingly, it has been found that moped enthusiasts are predominantly adults. Some mopeds go no faster than seventeen miles per hour; others may have maximum speeds ranging from eighteen to thirty miles per hour. Many youngsters do not find such low mileage per hour appealing. However, these rates are very appealing to adults who find mopeds very useful for commuting to work, going to the supermarket, traveling short distances for miscellaneous purposes, and also simply for fun. Many people are finding mopeds a great deal of fun as a means of transportation.

Since it is essential that mopeds be kept in good repair, the career of the *moped repairer* was born. There are many different brands of mopeds, most of which are European-manufactured. The dealers, in many cases, learn how to maintain and repair the moped which they sell. Thus, they may be *moped dealer–repairers*. There are also *motorcycle repairers* and *automobile repairers* who have learned to repair mopeds and thereby function also as moped repairers. With the increasing number of mopeds in the United States, there are a growing number

146

of moped repairers whose repair activities are concentrated on mopeds only or, at least, predominantly.

Moped repairers may repair and overhaul the vehicles as needed. They discuss with the customers the nature and extent of damage and/or malfunction. They perform such tasks as inspecting the vehicles, diagnosing the problems, overhauling the engines, and lubricating the vehicles. They examine the frames and hammer out dents and bends in them. These repairers listen to a moped motor's performance and dismantle and repair it according to necessity. They may repair and adjust the brakes and/or the pedals. They repair and replace defective parts as required.

Moped repairers should possess mechanical ability and be moped enthusiasts. They should be skilled in diagnosing a moped's mechanical and electrical problems. Present moped repairers, in the main, are mechanics who have learned their trade on the job. Vocational high school or technical school programs in automobile mechanics and motorcycle repair are valuable for those who would like to become moped repairers. Many of these programs are adding courses in small-engine repair and moped maintenance.

In view of the high cost of gasoline, more and more families are buying mopeds in place of second cars. The number of moped enthusiasts is on the rise and with this will come a growing need for moped repairers. For additional information about this new career, write to the Automotive Service Industry Association, 230 N. Michigan Ave., Chicago, Ill. 60601; the National Automobile Dealers Association, 2000 K St. N.W., Washington, D.C. 20006; and the aforementioned Motorized Bicycle Association.

For a free pamphlet on moped safety, write to the National Safety Council, 444 N. Michigan Ave., Chicago, Ill. 60611.

Fuel problems—high costs and shortages—are resulting in the creation of yet another vast new category of specialists. There is career "sunshine" in solar energy. The sun's roaring furnace offers tremendous potential as the basis for a future heating industry right here on earth.

The question many are asking is whether the sun will be able to provide us with a significant proportion of our energy needs. The answer seems to be yes. On the horizon, there is appearing an industry based on the use of solar energy for heating purposes. Solar heating is being described as one of our nation's "coming growth industries." However, this industry is still in its infancy.

As yet, solar units for home heating are expensive. The growth and expansion of the solar industry is dependent upon the mass production of solar equipment. Solar collectors are basic "hardware" in solar-heating systems. These collectors are panels that are placed on the roof or at the side of the house for the purpose of absorbing the sun's rays. Solar furnaces and special storage tanks are additional necessary hardware.

Solar-equipment technicians and *solar-heating salespersons* will need to be trained to understand this hardware. The continuing rise in energy (electricity, gas, petroleum) costs will also tend to speed the expansion of this industry.

A solar-energy corps trained in the field of solar technology will be added to our nation's work force as time goes on. *Solar-heating specialists,* predominantly *solar-*

heating engineers (or *solar engineers*) and *solar-heating scientists*, are the backbone of this new and growing industry. In addition to the solar engineers, who will devote all their time and energies in helping homeowner's and industry with their heating problems, there will be an ever increasing need for *solar-heating technicians* trained in solar technology to assist the solar engineers.

Other existing skilled workers, such as *carpenters, cement masons, crane operators, electricians, glaziers, plumbers, sheet-metal workers,* and miscellaneous factory workers, will enter the solar-heating field and acquire the additional knowledge and skill which will be required of them in this field. *Real-estate personnel* of varied types will also enter this field after becoming knowledgeable about solar heating.

Engineering curricula in four-year colleges and universities, and two-year engineering technology programs in junior and community colleges throughout the nation, are gradually adding courses in solar energy. Check with the school of your choice to determine whether or not solar energy has already been added to their courses of study.

As the solar-heating industry grows, it will offer employment opportunities to countless thousands of workers in new careers. If you would like to play a role in the solar-heating industry, write to the Energy Research and Development Administration, Washington, D.C. for further information. Additional information may also be obtained from the National Science Foundation, 1800 G St. N.W., Washington, D.C. 20550 and the National Solar Energy Education Campaign, 10762 Tucker St., Beltsville, Md. 20705.

12

You in the New, Unique Future

Many changes have taken place in the working world. Many changes will continue to take place. The years ahead will bring with them new industries not at all foreseeable now. These new industries will create new occupations. Additionally, new occupations will arise within existing industries and professions.

Our nation's population in 1977 was approximately 217 million with a labor force of about 97 million. It is expected that our population will be about 235 million and our labor force approximately 108 million in 1985.

Women constituted 40 percent of the 1977 labor force and this percentage has continued to rise with the passage of time.

Most of these additional workers will enter existing traditional occupations. Clerical workers will constitute the fastest growing occupational group. Opportunities for service workers will also increase rapidly. But, there will be new and unique opportunities for these workers too.

As time goes on, there will be more and greater pioneering of outer space. The space industry of the future will require a vast variety of highly skilled persons not only to build spaceships but also to maintain and repair all that will be involved in outer space and interplanetary travel and communications. Space colonization will call for the development of new careers; new skills and special knowledge will be essential.

Industries related to the production of energy will have more rapid growth than other industries. New specialists may arise in petroleum and natural-gas extraction, coal mining, atomic energy, and solar energy to meet the ever increasing need and demand for energy.

Another segment of our labor force that is expected to grow rapidly is the health-services industry. Greater numbers of physicians, nurses, and miscellaneous medical technologists and therapists will be required to treat patients. Our population is growing older and, generally, older people require more medical care and attention. New techniques will be developed to aid in the diagnosis and cure of varied illnesses, and new types of medical and health-services personnel will be needed for this.

Computers will be used more extensively and play increasingly important roles in business and scientific research. Not only will more systems analysts and programmers be needed, but new types of occupations will develop and specialized professional and technical personnel will be required for these occupations.

Technological innovations will bring about the creation of many new occupations totally unknown to us at present. Along with this will come the decline and possible disappearance of occupations now familiar to us. Although the number of professional and technical workers will rise rapidly in some expanding fields, college graduates will not necessarily be in favored positions throughout the labor market. The completion of two-year programs in community and junior colleges may be sufficient for entry into new paraprofessional and technical careers.

CAREERS NEW AND UNIQUE

The creation and development of new careers as a consequence of our ever advancing technology will make it necessary for many workers to return to the classrooms for additional training or for complete retraining for new careers. Adult-education programs will increase in popularity and enable workers to change from one career to another as needs, interests, and abilities dictate.

Adult-education specialists will be in demand and adult-education programs will flourish as older citizens seek more knowledge for vocational and avocational purposes. Specialized education will be the key to facilitate adaptation in a constantly changing and advancing world of work.

Changes in the working world may bring increased tensions and stresses to workers on all levels of the career ladders. Psychologists and other behavioral specialists will be needed to aid workers in reducing and coping with these pressures. Industrial psychologists will help to determine the causes of their stress and aid workers at their places of employment.

Workers of the future will have several different careers during their lifetimes. Vocational-guidance specialists will be needed to aid them in making appropriate career choices and in facilitating their transfer from one career to another.

The future will be dynamic, unique—and, of course, new. For you, individually, the future will be what you make of it. The opportunities will be there. It will be your task to seek them out.

If you desire it, train for it and seek it, the chances are good that, in your future, there will be a career—new and/or unique.

Sources of Further Information

There are references to sources of further information throughout this book. If you would like to read more about any one of the specific careers included in this book, contact or write to the respective sources and you will probably receive a miscellany of brochures and other career materials. It is also advisable that you write to the U.S. Department of Labor, Employment and Training Administration, Washington, D.C. 20213, for their latest career information about those careers which are of particular interest to you.

Since the careers discussed in this book are new and/or unique, in the main, entire books have not as yet been written about any of the specific, individual careers. It is suggested that you keep in touch with your school and public librarians and your school counselor to learn about new books on these careers as they are published.

The following books, published by the publisher of this book, are, to some degree, pertinent to the subject of new and unique careers and, therefore, merit your attention:

Dowdell, Dorothy, and Dowdell, Joseph, *Careers in Horticultural Sciences.* 1975.

Duckat, Walter, *A Guide to Professional Careers.* 1970.

Lee, Essie E., *Careers in the Health Field.* 1974.

Liston, Robert A., *On the Job Training and Where to Get It.* 1973.

Science Book Associates, *Careers in the Earth Sciences.* 1975.

Science Books Associates, *Careers in Environmental Protection.* 1974.

Science Book Associates, *Challenging Careers in Urban Affairs.* 1976.

Searight, Mary W., *Your Career in Nursing.* 1978.

Splaver, Sarah, *Career Choices in Psychology.* 1976.

Splaver, Sarah, *Nontraditional Careers for Women.* 1973.

Splaver, Sarah, *Nontraditional College Routes to Careers.* 1975.

Splaver, Sarah, *Paraprofessions: Careers of the Future and the Present.* 1972.

Splaver, Sarah, *You and Today's Troubled World.* 1970.

Splaver, Sarah, *Your Career—If You're Not Going to College.* 1971.

Splaver, Sarah, *Your Handicap—Don't Let It Handicap You.* 1974.

Splaver, Sarah, *Your Personality and Your Career.* 1977.

Index

ABOUT THE AUTHOR

Sarah Splaver is a noted guidance consultant and counseling psychologist. She holds a Master of Arts degree from Teachers College, Columbia University, and a Doctor of Philosophy degree from New York University. She served for several years as a high school Director of Guidance. She is nationally and internationally well known as the originator of the socioguidrama, a group guidance technique used as a means of helping young people with their problems.

Dr. Splaver is licensed as a registered psychologist by the Department of Education of the state of New York. She has served as a consultant on psychological and guidance projects to the U.S. Department of Health, Education and Welfare; U.S. Defense Department; Department of the Army; New York Life Insurance Company; International Business Machines Corp; and various other organizations. She has counseled thousands of college-bound and non-college-bound young people and adults. As a consultant, she has worked on computerized guidance programs.

Her articles on guidance, psychology, and career information have appeared in professional journals and other publications. She has authored dozens of *Occupational Abstracts,* prepared the *Guide to Career Literature* for the New York Life Insurance Company's Career Information Service, and written many books and playlets in the field of guidance and psychology. She has lectured at conferences, young people's gatherings, and parent-teacher and other meetings. She is the former Director of *Guidance Exchange.*

Dr. Splaver is a Life Member of the American Personnel and Guidance Association. Among the other professional organizations in which she holds membership are the National Vocational Guidance Association, American School Counselor Association, American Psychological Association, International Council of Psychologists, American Rehabilitation Counseling Association, Association for Religious and Value Issues in Counseling, American Association for the Advancement of Science, and the Authors Guild.

CONTENTS

SHERRI GELDIN

FOREWORD

When Carlos Basualdo presented Jeanne van Heeswijk's proposal, *Face Your World*, as part of his *Notations* series, I confess to a vague discomfort. Was there not a long history of discredited projects where well-intended experiments sought to press art into service as an instrument for social change? Had we not come to learn that the arts change life more circuitously, by reflecting the hidden truths of ourselves back to us as through a mirror? I, for one, felt firm in the conviction that as we come to know ourselves ever more subtly through the arts, we become ever more supple to the benefits of those more direct tools of social change: law, policy, and political action. Art changes life surely and certainly, but only as Art. Yet now, Jeanne van Heeswijk proposed to outfit a bus and literally hit the streets to engage and interact with inner-city children, to affect their lives in the name of and through art. Another young artist, confident, earnest, and fiercely committed to a social ideal that I worried would elude her.

But I was very wrong. The more I studied *Face Your World*, the more I realized just how much intelligence van Heeswijk brought to bear in her effort to revisit the possibilities of art as a social instrument. Every dimension of the project, from the colorful graphics of the bus exterior to the friendly monster bus stops designed by her artist/architect colleague Joep van Lieshout, to the playful computer game designed to captivate kids with the challenges of city planning, spoke to the light but savvy touch she would exercise as she conjured a child's-eye view of the world. Perhaps most compelling was the concept behind the Interactor software program, designed with Maaike Engelen and a team of ingenious collaborators at V2_Organisation in Rotterdam. In the interactive play of *Face Your World*, children take pictures of themselves and their surroundings with digital cameras, merge them with some five hundred local images already embedded in the program, and then collectively play with them, moving them here and there, changing their world and themselves in the process. The game never directs or even attempts to persuade the kids of this or that better life but simply encourages them to imagine and then reimagine the context in which they find themselves. Or as Carlos observes later in this publication, "to make their imagination produce the very possibility of change… [through] the very possibility of collective invention." *Face Your World* thus enabled the children to take a small but essential step along the transformative path of self-awareness. Clearly, van Heeswijk had more than learned the lessons of history; she had brilliantly conceived of a way to place art's greatest power in the hands of children.

There are so many forces that come into play in order to realize a project of this creative scope and ambition. In fact, the word "collaboration" barely seems adequate to describe the exceptional network of partners, inside and outside the Wexner Center, who brought their talents and tenacity to bear. We are especially grateful to Greater Columbus Arts Council President Ray Hanley; Timothy Katz, Program Director for Community Arts Education at GCAC; and Jim Arter, Associate Artist with the Children of the Future program. Our partners at GCAC in turn initiated and facilitated our interface with three inner-city venues: Blackburn Recreation Center, Sawyer Recreation Center, and the Boys & Girls Clubs of Columbus Westside Unit. Our thanks also go to Wayne Roberts, Director of the Columbus Recreation and Parks Department, and Molly Frank of the Boys & Girls Clubs of Columbus, under whose leadership these sites are activated for the benefit of area children. In addition, we deeply appreciate the collaboration of the individual Children of the Future artist members at the three sites and, of course, the creative contributions of all the participating children, listed on the inside of the front cover.

Special recognition and gratitude are due to Ronald L. Barnes, President and CEO of COTA, whose enthusiastic embrace of *Face Your World* was overwhelming. Barnes's enlightened view of public service made possible the crucial donation of a COTA bus that could be entirely retrofitted with computer stations and transformed into a mobile digital art studio. Max Moore, Project Coordinator for Mayor Michael B. Coleman's

Downtown Business Plan, generously lent his urban planning expertise to the project and his name to the avatar in *Face Your World*'s Interactor game.

We are fortunate to have the multiple insights – about the project and van Heeswijk's unique place in the art world – offered by catalogue essayists Carlos Basualdo, Reinaldo Laddaga, Steven Hunt, Maaike Engelen, and Vesta A. H. Daniel and Cynthia Collins. Graphic designer Roger Teeuwen realized the striking design of the publication as a complement to the lively graphic identity he developed for the project as a whole. We appreciate his visual contributions, as well as those of Rolf Engelen, whose photographs figure prominently in both the book and the Interactor.

The artist's principal collaborators at V2_Lab, International Lab for the Unstable Media (the research and development wing of V2_Organisation), were nothing short of amazing in their design of the Interactor, the software program that fuels *Face Your World*. Theirs was truly an instrumental and defining role, as was that of creative programmer Marco Christis. The anthropomorphic bus stops that greet the children as they arrive at the three sites, replete with facial monitors to reflect the progress of the game, are the inspired creation of Atelier van Lieshout, with special thanks to artist Joep van Lieshout for his willingness to play a fellow artist's game. The furnishings for the interior of the bus were fabricated by Matt Clausen.

Within the Wexner Center itself, a wide range of talent joined forces with van Heeswijk: first and foremost the curatorial team of Carlos Basualdo and Steven Hunt, who expertly shepherded a complex collaboration to fruition, along with trusted assistant Kelly Merryman. Steve, in particular, deserves our boundless appreciation for his daily diligence over so many months. We are also pleased to recognize educators Patricia Trumps, Cynthia Collins, Kendra Girardot, Chris Hutchins, design director Jeffrey M Packard, editor Ann Bremner, and communications director Darnell Lautt for their many contributions to the project. Technicians

Stephen Jones, Mike Sullivan, Larry "Pug" Heller, Paul Jones, David Bamber, and Benjamin Knepper, along with their captains James A. Scott and John A. Smith, were indispensable to its success. And we are grateful for the administrative support provided to the project by Gretchen Metzelaars, Jeffrey Kipnis, and Jill Davis.

It is always a pleasure to highlight the generosity of our sponsors in such an endeavor, and we are proud to have enlisted significant support from the Greater Columbus Arts Council, along with exceptional in-kind support from COTA and the Children of the Future program. We are also fortunate for the partnership of the Mondriaan Foundation, Amsterdam; the Consulate General of the Netherlands in New York; and the Corporate Annual Fund of the Wexner Center Foundation. As ever, I am grateful to the foundation trustees for their unwavering commitment to the Wexner Center's laboratory mission – one that allows projects like *Face Your World* to germinate and thrive.

Finally, I extend my enormous admiration and gratitude to Jeanne van Heeswijk, who has conceived and achieved a truly remarkable intervention, one that conveys the transformative powers of art to eager young minds. The Wexner Center is proud to have played a part in forging that magical link.

Sherri Geldin
Director, Wexner Center for the Arts

Miracle·Gro
Kids of Columbus
A partnership with the
Scotts Miracle-Gro
Foundation and
The Neighborhood
House, Inc.

INTRODUCTION
FACE IT

Beauty is the result of a collective action of liberation that presents itself as pure excess of being. – Toni Negri, *Art and Multitude*

Jeanne van Heeswijk's *Face Your World* is part of *Notations*, a series of exhibitions that borrows its title from the homonymous book by John Cage and constitutes an attempt to articulate at the level of exhibition-making several of the theoretical postulates that Cage's work and writing exemplified. The series arose from both a wish to interpellate the mandate inscribed in the Peter Eisenman building that houses the Wexner Center for the Arts and an acknowledgment of the similarities between the Wexner Center's architectural and cultural program and that of Cage's work.

Inscribed in the narrow angle between the grid of the city of Columbus and that of The Ohio State University campus, while at the same time sitting firmly on the latter's ground, the Eisenman project is a permanent reminder of the position that cultural production occupies in contemporary life. Morphologically, the Eisenman building alludes both to the past of Ohio State – through the schematic reference to the towers of an old armory building that once was part of the university – and to the regenerative possibilities of culture in the design and fabric of the social tissue: the white grid that signifies scaffolding as a sign of the permanently incomplete and unending character of cultural production.

Located between the campus and the city, between present and past, permanence and mutability, the Eisenman building poses a clear challenge to the Wexner Center: the need to activate the interstitial spaces that structure social and cultural production by means of an unending process of reinvention of contemporary culture and its role in society.

Cage's *Notations* was both an exhibition of a diverse variety of musical scores by an international group of contemporary artists and musicians and a spontaneous but thorough presentation of the new developments in the visual arts and music of his time. Cage conceived his book in the intersection between the visual arts, musical experimentation, and exhibition practice – as a graphic demonstration of the inextricable links between those disciplines in modern culture. Just like the Wexner Center building, Cage's *Notations* operate in the space between fixed definitions, reinventing and reinscribing them in their original context in such a way as to redefine that context.

The goal of this series of exhibitions is to reread productively the cultural program inscribed in the building, departing from the practices of a group of international contemporary artists whose work is committed to the unraveling of the distances between disciplines and engaged in the production of an experimental form of knowledge that is fundamentally cross-disciplinary and socially minded. At the same time, these presentations aim to activate links between the Wexner Center and the larger Columbus community, establishing a closer relationship with the university while at the same time exploring nontraditional exhibition spaces and situations. Internally, the series also encourages collaboration among the different departments that constitute the center and a horizontal, nonhierarchical integration of its constituency.

Face Your World, a collaboration between the Wexner Center, the Central Ohio Transit Authority (COTA), and the Children of the Future program of the Greater Columbus Arts Council (GCAC) is the ideal platform to realize many of the postulates of *Notations* as a series. The project was conceived in a dialogue between the curatorial and the education departments at the Wexner Center, and staff from both departments worked closely with the artist in its realization.

The implications of the project's title, *Face Your World*, are clearly twofold. On the one hand the expression results from a clear interpellation to its participatory audience: Stand for yourselves and see for yourselves the place where you are, where you act. And by doing that, appropriate that reality, make it yours. The "world" that van Heeswijk alludes to in

the title of her project is in fact made of the harsh realities
of inner cities in the United States. The city of Columbus
becomes then, in this sense, almost a textbook case, with a
fragile public education system, an inner city scarred by
petty crime, little efficient public housing, pockets of chronic
unemployment, and what constitutes de facto racial
segregation. That is, in fact, the world that van Heeswijk
herself attempts to confront with her project while making
her audience confront it as well. A world that, like it or not,
clearly belongs to the audience – both in the sense that they
are part of it and that they have, by virtue of that pertinence,
the possibility to modify it.

But *Face Your World* also implies the possibility of giving a
face to those living conditions, harsh as they are. A face, in
this context, is nothing but a synonym for subjective agency,
and van Heeswijk is again inviting her audience to, properly
speaking, give their actions and their imagination the form of
an agency. What is proper to a face is its capacity to express,
and thus, to communicate. A face expresses not only through
language, but more importantly, through emotions. It could
even be said that a face is that very potential to express
something that can not be satisfactorily uttered with words,
it is communication before meaning. It is, more precisely, the
communication of the pure fact of being that comes before
and ultimately shapes meaning as such. As is the case with
any face, the title of this project is itself an interpellation:
make a map of feelings in your world, map your world with
your feelings, and imagine how to change the world and
the map, inventing new meanings. Ultimately, a face is like
a collection of images yet unseen, and it is through the
production of images that van Heeswijk invites the recipients
of her invocation to become the owners of their meanings.

As described throughout this book, *Face Your World* is
intended to allow a group of children ages five to twelve to
produce their own images of their surroundings by using
computer software called the Interactor and developed by
van Heeswijk in collaboration with poet and philosopher

Maaike Engelen and a group of software designers from the city of Rotterdam – V2_Lab. The software is installed in a number of computers inside a small COTA bus, which is used to take the kids around the city of Columbus, functioning simultaneously as an exploration tool and an urban laboratory for the imagination. The results of the children's work, a collection of personalized images of imaginary public spaces, are displayed on three "bus stops," which are in fact slightly anthropomorphic public sculptures, designed by another van Heeswijk collaborator, the Dutch artist Joep van Lieshout and his Atelier van Lieshout.

This is the point where it becomes relevant to consider what is properly "artistic" about this project that seems so multi-faceted and close to other disciplines, such as sociology or education, or that may even represent a chapter of an imaginary anthropology of the self. This is the fact that *Face Your World* operates through images. The dimension of excess is always implicated in the image (excess of meaning, to start with, as images are always that which escapes the very possibility of being signified) and is precisely what authorizes its audience of users to appropriate their world while they produce it. This appropriation is, of course, not entirely factual. The audience – but it might be better to refer to them as "actors," as their participation in the project is an extremely active one – is not intended to reconstruct the actual city, but to imagine the very possibility of doing that. To imagine that, precisely through the production of a number of images, or, to put it differently, to make their imagination produce the very possibility of change. What makes this project "artistic" may be that it operates primarily through a dimension that could be better described as metaphoric. What it creates is, first and foremost, the very possibility of collective invention.

This might be described as one of the major concerns of a number of contemporary artists: how to operate in reality while at the same time maintaining the independence that seems to be one of the major achievements of modernity.

Or, to better express it, how to maintain a certain degree of
autonomy while at the same time producing effects in reality.
In that sense *Face Your World* is a clear indication of the
present state of things. The project is an invitation to act,
but to act through images, to produce images that act.
A metaphor, undoubtedly, but one with tangible effects.

The possibility of maintaining a certain degree of
independence – of the determinations of the market, as is
often the case, but also of the restrictions of the institutions
of art, and of artistic practice as an institution as well – while
at the same time producing a set of tangible effects seems to
necessitate the constitution of an intermediate body that both
articulates the work and makes it possible. It is, in other words,
through the invention of a dimension of commonality that
this specific work functions. This is the point where the
audience may cease to be passive and become instead a set
of actors, who are – as Maaike Engelen clearly describes in
her text – by necessity interconnected. What is needed for
the work to be realized is a "nest," in the words of Reinaldo
Laddaga, also a contributor to this catalogue, or an imagined
form of collective agency. Steve Hunt refers to this issue in
detail in his essay, analyzing a possible genealogy of collective
agency in seventeenth-century Dutch group portraiture.
Vesta A. H. Daniel and Cynthia Collins take the discussion
in a slightly different direction, focusing on the connections
van Heeswijk has made in the Columbus community. And
although Engelen focuses on the theoretical implications
of the software and Laddaga traces the itinerary of van
Heeswijk's practice, both of them also end up interrogating
this particular aspect of the artist's practice, in sum, the fact
that van Heeswijk's worlds are, first and foremost, possible
communities. It could even be said that *Face Your World* is
a poetic proposal for the constitution of a community that,
beginning as an experiment in relating a number of different
constituencies in a given city, would end as a collection of
images, which are in turn capable of generating a future
community of viewers.

If one would take *Face Your World* for what it is as an artwork
and for what it attempts to do in reality and use it as a vantage
point to define a wide range of contemporary artistic practices,
one would have to conclude that art is that form of collective
action by which a community is invented as a metaphor.
More than the images themselves, what would remain after
the project is concluded will possibly be the metaphor of the
community that produced them.

Carlos Basualdo
Curator, *Face Your World*

FACE YOUR WORLD
FACE YOUR WORLD
STOP
FACE
YOU

WORLD
FACE YOUR WORLD
POLICE

YOUR MO

2010

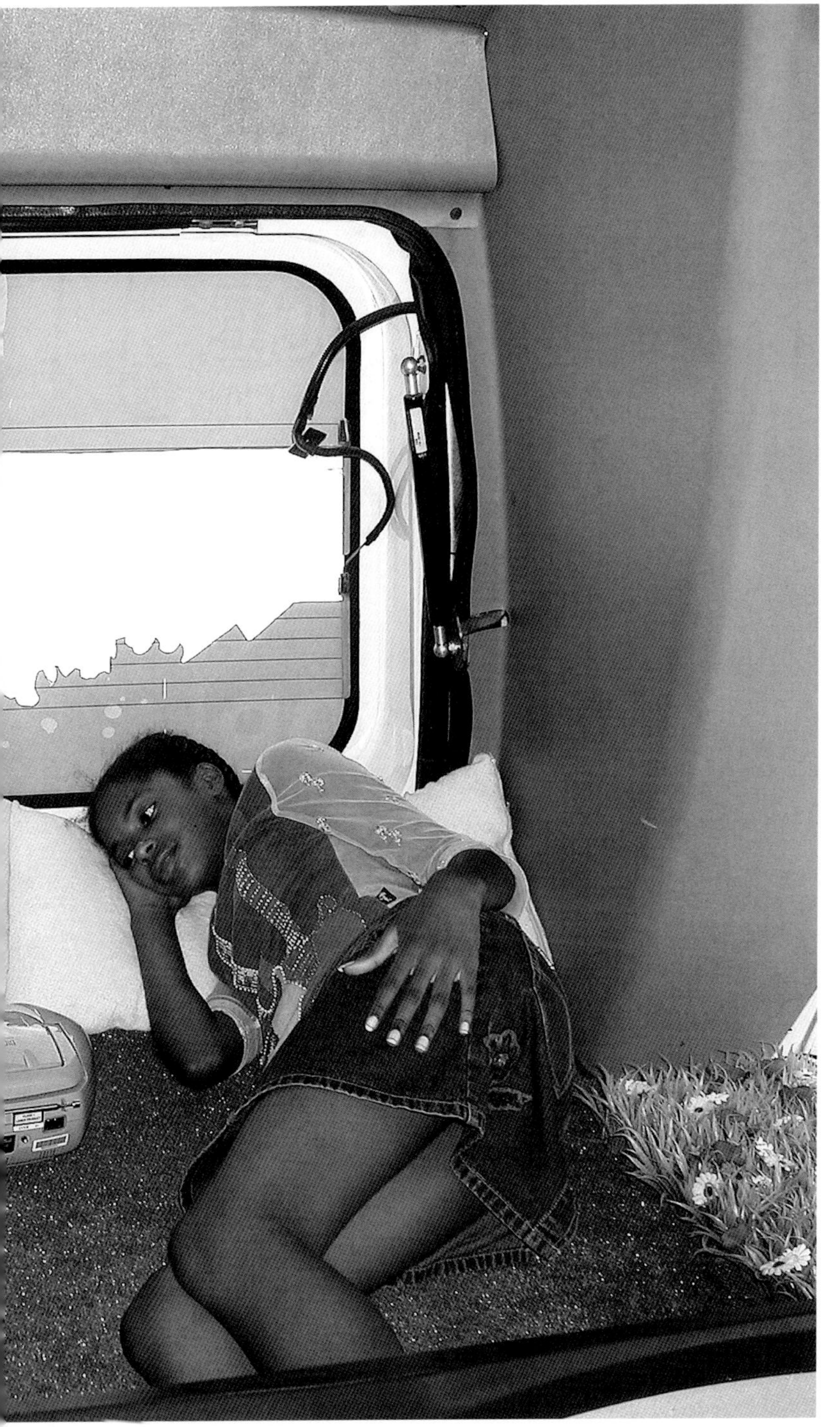

FACE YOUR WORLD
POLICE
low
Donahue Pizza

2010

NETWORKS, FACES, MEMBRANES

I.

In 1993, Jeanne van Heeswijk installed in her studio a mobile room that she had just finished building: a simple cube of light wood, which could be assembled and disassembled, implanted and transported. She called it **Room with a View**. The interior walls of the cube were covered in drawings, texts, and objects, and some two dozen artists, critics, and curators were invited to discuss with her the concept that had given rise to the project. To discuss this concept, and also the problem of private and public spaces – which proved particularly appropriate, if you consider that the **Room**, in its later installations, would configure itself as a kind of an enclave of privacy in a public space, whether in a room at the Rheinische Landklinik, in Kleve, Germany, or in the former departure hall of the Holland-Amerika Line, in Rotterdam. These conversations were not recorded or documented, but when they were over the artist produced a poster, on which a simple caption could be read: "Private faces in public places are wiser and nicer than public faces in private places." (The phrase is a quotation from W. H. Auden.)

In 1996, on the occasion of **Manifesta 1** in Rotterdam, Jeanne van Heeswijk initiated a temporary association with the name of **NEsTWORK**.[1] It consisted of a group of seven people who developed an extensive series of activities during the exhibition (performances, concerts, lectures, and films), all focusing on the notion of the "local." Once again, her

Room with a View, *Plaatsbepaling*, 1996
Room, dancer
With Susan Kozel
Museum voor Moderne Kunst, Arnhem

Room with a View, *Dependance*, 1994
Room, actress
With Anke van der Pluijm
Art Fair, Amsterdam

1. NEsTWORK is Karin Arink, Wapke Feenstra, Jeanne van Heeswijk, Edwin Janssen, Menna Laura Meijer, Kamiel Verschuren, Ruud Welten.

Office of NEsTWORK, 1996
CBK (Center of Visual Arts), Rotterdam

In 1997, Jeanne van Heeswijk recorded a series of conversations with artists and with students in the M.A. in Creative Curating course at Goldsmiths College, London. The theme? "The silence between things and the necessity to take breaks."[2] The title of the piece? ***Break. Dance.*** Let us insert this title in our little chain of equivalents: A private face in a public place is like a nest in a network, is like a silence between things and a break in a dance, is like…

intent was the opening of a space of conversation, where images could be generated at the same time as discourses are developed, and where the aim was the establishment of a mode of connection with the site where these generations and developments would take place. And once again, within the name of the operation or the piece (piece, operation, program: all these names and others could be given to van Heeswijk's interventions), there was an expression establishing a link between an exteriority and an interiority. A nest in a network. A private face in a public place. Are the two relations equivalent? Perhaps not. But perhaps they are, which would be more intriguing. A private face in a public place is like a nest in a network, is like…

This chain of equivalents marks off the territory in which van Heeswijk's work unfolds. But in what sense? What is there in common between a break in a dance, a nest in a network, and a private face in a public space? Interrupt, enclose, exhibit: what kind of action is formed through this chain? Van Heeswijk's work can be understood as a meditation on these equivalents, a meditation that is not conducted

2. The conversations were subsequently edited by the artist and then sampled and mixed by composer Johnny Clark. They were converted into an installation, a CD, and a "live re-mix event": the norm for van Heeswijk is that there is no action that does not result in a form to be sent and received, extended or compressed, that cannot become the object of a circulation.

in solitude, but out in the world (but what can it mean here, "out in the world"?). A meditation that is conducted even as the occupation of certain places, the configuration of certain circuits, the implantation of certain images, and the invitation to certain conversations takes place.

And why all of this?

II.

I receive an envelope from the artist. The envelope includes some of her texts. One of them is called "Fleeting images of community."[3] The text is simple and clear: a chain of assertions about what, in her judgment, would be possible (and even necessary) these days, for art in general. What is the situation in which, according to her, artistic proposals take place? "In a time where specialization continues to increase, there is little space left to really connect things such as the communication between various disciplines and between various subcultures. It appears to be close to impossible to bridge the various social islands" (175). Can art do something to deal with the situation? Yes, she believes. Why? "The interesting aspect of visual art is its relatively autonomous position, which provides a sanctuary where new things can emerge" (175). Beginning from the territories of art, it is possible to establish platforms making certain encounters possible. "The direct attention in my work for the participant implies the creation of platforms where people are able to encounter each other again and design and represent their own environment" (175). Not that these are two separate things: the encounter, on one hand, and the design and representation of the environment, on the other. It is a matter of creating "platforms" (more-or-less established sites that, at the same time, are launch sites), where it would be possible for anyone to construct representations of the environment on the basis of the meeting that takes place – and at the same time, to represent the environment in such a way as to encourage the extension and consolidation of the meeting.

3. Jeanne van Heeswijk, "Fleeting images of community," in Anette Balkema and Henk Slager (eds.), "Exploding Aesthetics," *Lier en Boog* vol. 16 (Amsterdam, Atlanta: Rodopi, 2001), 175–178. Page references for quotations are given parenthetically in the text.

This is why art, these days, is not simply a matter of proposing solutions to aesthetic problems. "One should attempt to formulate a new moral attitude, since I don't believe in an aesthetics without ethics" (175). The space of art should be one where "a new moral attitude might be formulated" (175). A new moral attitude? What sort of attitude? "Such a moral attitude should embrace the pluriformity of our contemporary society and attempt to escape from both relativism and fundamentalism. At the same time, it has to focus on the necessity of creating contexts outside of recognized art spaces while breaking down the isolated positions of these spaces" (175–176). It is a matter of constructing an "interstitial space," where the formation of these modes of relation can be verified, taking into account the fact that the relations are always mediated and give rise to what van Heeswijk calls "agglutinations": temporary fixations of elements susceptible of being exhibited.

The idea is to constitute such a space from the general region of the "visual arts." For no matter how far the works can be taken in the discursive domain, the artist – van Heeswijk says – does not act as a "cultural theorist." Why? Because "imagination and the space for the image continue to be decisive" (177). The image? No doubt because it partakes of an anarchic exception, an event that takes place beyond all particular conditions, bearing with it the marks of its singular emergence. Of course it is not only a matter of proposing images, but of investigating "the conditions under which images could be regenerated" (178). Because images, each of them, and the culture of the image in which they are produced, must be regenerated. Why? "I believe that today's aesthetics has isolated art by separating image from reality, while shifting presentation to representation. Because of that, isolated images have emerged without any connection to reality. In my work, I try to create contexts for images and different possibilities so that images have the capacity to reconnect in a meaningful way to their environment" (178). And in what ways is this done? "In order to explore those kinds of questions, my activities are primarily focused on constructing frameworks. Then I guide the processes happening inside that frame, although I don't enforce anything. At the most, I create conditions where moments could emerge which intervene with perception, so that new images or frameworks might come into being. However, because the 'anything goes' principle has led to super-differentiation and non-communication in various domains, once in a while frameworks have to be closed" (178). This recognition that "once in a while frameworks have to be closed" is what is meant, among other things, in the title of one of van Heeswijk's works: *Draw a Line*.[4]

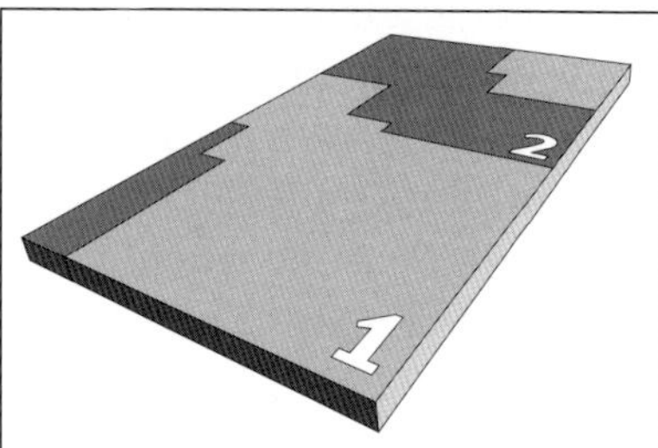
Jeanne van Heeswijk, *Draw a Line*, 2000
Wood, sand
206 $\frac{1}{4}$ x 206 $\frac{1}{4}$ inches (524 x 524 cm)
Courtesy of the Tokyo Opera City Art Gallery

4. In 2000, van Heeswijk was invited to participate in the *Territory* exhibition at the Tokyo Opera City Art Gallery. She proposed the project *Draw a Line*, which is based on an old Dutch game. Van Heeswijk describes the project in this way: "In collaboration with Rolf Engelen an area of twenty-five square meters was filled with earth in the gallery which referred to the Dutch tradition of land reclamation. In the gallery the game 'landjepik' could be played, which centers on gaining and losing territory, land, and space. By alternately throwing a knife in one of the parts of the area of land, the two players try to gain parts of each other's territory. The work was accompanied by a booklet with the rules of the game that can be played in three varieties, 'Wanna play,' 'Wanna fight,' and 'Wanna act.' In the latter variation the assignment is to create space for the opposition instead of taking space away from them; an impossible assignment in a game of conquering." But maybe the most common assignment in the games van Heeswijk proposes…

"Draw a line": how to draw a line? How to do it in such a way that the more-or-less reserved space this drawing establishes, rather than being a cloistered preserve, is a platform on the basis of which the other, friend or enemy, can be approached in full uncertainty? Such a thing appears particularly important, to her eyes, at a moment like ours: because it is true that artistic proposals deal with the concrete condition of the present described here as "super-differentiation."

III.

"Super-differentiation." What does it mean? No doubt what a certain tradition of social thought considers as the decisive trait of modernity, the propensity of modern societies to differentiate themselves into subsystems: a political system differentiated from a religious system, an economic system differentiated from a legal system, and, of course, an art system with its own particular objectives and ways of proceeding. This process then opens up a space for the will to autonomy that has been characteristic of art under the conditions of modernity, an autonomy to which van Heeswijk's practice bears

ambiguous allegiance. For it is not a matter, in her view, of remaining faithful to an art that proposes to create objects unfolding within a sphere separated by a distinct line from the one in which individuals carry out their daily practices, practices of action and conversation, of consent and exchange. But nor is she interested in participating in that specific type of rebellion against the institutions of the modernity that can still be identified as the neo-avant-garde, insofar as the latter aspired to an excessively simple fusion of art and life. Van Heeswijk aspires to develop her work through a complex play of distancing and interchange, which involves a strategic affirmation of certain aspects of the tradition of autonomy – at least insofar as that tradition involves a space of reserve for the taking of decisions that give rise to gestures that can create distance from our own present, and resituate life as it is within the framework of life as it could be – while also allowing images to be "reconnected" to their "environments." Autonomy, in short, as "a sanctuary where new things can emerge" – even if these things bear little resemblance to what modernity had consecrated as art.

But I suspect that when van Heeswijk speaks of "super-differentiation" she does not only refer to these artistic questions, but also to what happens in the present to the individuals in those parts of the world where her work takes place (almost always regions of conflict and disintegration in the developed world). The present, considered in this respect as an epoch in the history of subjectivity, is characterized by the weakening of the forms of collective belonging that had defined late modernity: belonging to a nation, class, union, or party, to a religion or family, a form of belonging that constrained and connected one in a particular way. But there is also a particular constraint and connection for the individual who, in the world of "flexible labor," for example, experiences a gain in autonomy and mobility, but is also thrown entirely back on him- or herself, on his or her sheer particularity (as chance occurrence, as pure accident), a little like those "isolated images" of which van Heeswijk speaks, exposed to all the connections, but also to all the disasters. "Super-differentiation" means

this: the situation of an epoch when all the institutions and patterns which in the world of the modern had provided average individuals with forms of assurance and more-or-less recognizable limits have disintegrated, leaving large populations at the mercy of a strictly empty exteriority, where they can be captured by phobic programs that give an archaic name to the obscure anxieties they generate: the name of *security*.

This individual from the world of "super-differentiation" is the site in which new stakes come into play; and art can participate in this game, but only to the extent that it finds the resources. For this attenuation of collective belonging occurs at the same time as ever-wider networks of globalization arise. And with them arises a certain structure of feeling: one that derives from a sudden consciousness of global continuity, bringing the promise of a presence to each other as human beings – a co-presence quite outside the contexts that defined the same and the other under the conditions of late modernity – and at the same time, bringing the knowledge that humanity itself is a temporary and unstable result (and thus confronting us with a decision about the very definition of this humanity).

At the same time…

At one and the same time there is increasing individualization and increasing connection: a reduction of everyone to his or her sheer particularity, and an exposure to the other, to the human as such, in full uncertainty. But this situation offers the art of the present new challenges, at least if it seeks to connect itself to the epoch's sources of anxiety and invention. And it is here, in reflection on this situation, that van Heeswijk's work begins. For this reason, each time, in each local situation, her work is an answer to the repeated question: In a given situation, how to intervene in such a way that the people who are there can increase the number and intensity of their tics?

IV.

Nothing is more characteristic of van Heeswijk's works than the double gesture we can read in them: a gesture of rupture and reparation, of perturbation and quiescence, of imbalance and stabilization. As though it were necessary to advance polemically and yet at the same time to hold back, if indeed one wishes, from the territory of art, to approach that which in the world of "super-differentiation" appears both as a problem and a solution. "Super-differentiation" is characteristic of an epoch that sees both the constitution of a global scene and the dissolution of all the modernist formulas: the formulas for the inter-pretation of art, of the social, and of the relation between the two. But it is also an epoch that sees a decisive modification in modernity's figure of the subject.

Because the present is an epoch in which the image of the subject that modernity had taken for granted loses all its obviousness, from the field of legal or economic calculation to that of scientific or political representation, by way of the artistic culture that van Heeswijk suddenly finds incapable of offering that which it most lacks (platforms upon which meetings can take place, connections between images and environments, membranes that are at once permeable and protected). Modern art had addressed itself to and tacitly taken as its objective a subject that it assumed to be solidly installed within its own reserve, distancing itself from the field of objectivities, structured as the sum of a series of more-or-less separate subsystems all assembled in a more-or-less well-adjusted way.[5]

Van Heeswijk's practice, on the contrary, is designed for a subject who is always already inserted into an environment over which that subject tries to establish some control, seeing and hearing at the same time as doing. A subject in whom action and perception "interanimate": a subject who acts out a series of minimal actions to adjust her perceptions, while adjusting her perceptions to recommence her actions. Who travels to perceive, even if the journey is only a few yards long; and who perceives to compose a position from which a journey can begin again. At the same time…

5. This is why at a certain moment (it might be called the "formalist" moment) art seems to have addressed a subject which was no more than pure eye, seeing without touch or language; which in turn is why the first reactions to these positions so often took the form of an assertion of apocalyptic corporeality, the corporeality of a body without organs, and of language approaching the sob or the scream; an assertion of the body as an exorbitant outside, of language as a euphoric flux, of the image as a receptacle of pure force.

At the same time, this subject speaks, in order to establish a space of commonness with others: with the goal of separating out a platform, situating it within a network, bringing forth what is inherent in the place where it has been established, and sending whatever can be transmitted of this place through some circuit. This interanimation of perceptions and actions is also an interanimation of perceptions, actions, and discourses. Perceive, act, speak: the interplay is constant. For this reason all of van Heeswijk's proposals consist of stage-sets, programs, and incitements to conversation: constructing a cube, covering it with images, inviting some people to speak, publishing the dialogues, defining a system of exhibition and transport. Or defining a program that allows people to reconstruct their images of the city, inserting this program in computers, installing the computers in a bus, defining a circulation, proposing sites of exhibition. Perturbation and association, localization and transport, at the same time…

At the same time, all this is proposed to subjects who compose their own worlds articulated with thousands of mediators. For the idea is not only that the production of experiences be realized through the interactivation of perceptions, actions, and speech, but that this interactivation should also come into a circuit with fragments of the outside world, in a machine of knowledge, emotion, and association that, for each individual, is made not only of parts of her own body, but also of parts of her environment. Andy Clark calls "wideware" these fragments of the environment that adhere to or break off from the subject (adhering to, and at the same time, breaking off), that connect and disconnect her images. He asserts that "it is thus something of a question whether we should see the cognizer as the bare biological organism (that exploits all those external props and structures), or the organism-plus-wideware. To adopt the latter perspective is to opt for a kind of 'extended phenotype' view of the mind, in which the relation between the biological organism and the wideware is as important and intimate as that of the spider and the web."[6] Like a spider and its web.

A web that is increasingly populated by creatures of the digital universe. Because this epoch of "super-differentiation" is also the epoch when life unfolds through the thousand mediations of the digital, with its "props and structures," with all its modes of connecting images and environments. Van Heeswijk's practice takes place in a moment when all important art has to recognize that it is produced under conditions of digitalization: when every phenomenon appears, immediately, as a decomposable and recombinable transmission; when every subject receives every transmission as being susceptible of decomposition and recombination, at the same time…

At the same time as constant simulations unfold in her mind, at the same time as ongoing scenarios are spun out in her mind. For this is a subject who continually resituates what appears in what might appear: a subject who projects possible worlds into the slightest fissures in the real… But such a subject

6. Andy Clark, *Mindware: An Introduction to the Philosophy of Cognitive Science* (New York: Oxford University Press, 2000), 274.

requires new formations of art: and to begin, it requires that art reach beyond the paradigm of the object, if the object is a more-or-less compact appearance, with more-or-less well-defined edges, which appears by distinguishing itself more-or-less clearly from an individual who receives it in her distance and retreat. Instead of this, it requires that art turn to the construction of entities like those that van Heeswijk has been proposing for years: agglomerates of images, programs of action, means of transmission, and places that are offered to individuals less as things to be seen and analyzed than as nets in which they can take their places, somewhat like a spider in its web.

V.

Van Heeswijk, I assume, conceives of art as a moment in the more general project of the invention of a new culture for the left. An invention at once of an ethics, an aesthetics, and a new link between the two. And she knows, moreover, that the invention of a culture does not simply consist in the construction of systems of ideas, but also of architecture, of modes of connection and transport, of

canals and dikes, of continuities and interruptions. Modes of articulating interiorities and exteriorities, for example, in such a way that our most common notions of public and private are transformed.

From 1994 to 1998, in Overschie, van Heeswijk carried out a project with the title ***Buitenshuiskamer***

Jeanne van Heeswijk, *Buitenshuiskamer*, 1994–1998
Pots, plants, lamps
Mookhoekplein, Overschie, Rotterdam

(Outside livingroom). Between two seniors' residences was a glass-covered passageway. In cooperation with the inhabitants of the home, the passageway was furnished as a living room; it was supposed to remain only a couple of weeks, but it stayed for several years.

From 1996 to 2001, in the town hall of Oud-Beijerland, van Heeswijk, "in close collaboration with the architect Victor van Leeuw, constructed atmosphere zones, or so-called 'habitats,' that visualize what is going on in Oud-Beijerland and make the users of the building feel more at home" (her words). Note the similarity between visualization

and inhabitation, the link between a way of settling and a way of seeing, the combination of the house and the observatory, the house as observatory… And so the chain of equivalents extends: A private face in a public place is like a nest in a network, is like a silence between things and a break in a dance, is like a living room in a landscape, is like a habitat in a town hall, is like…

An "involution."

Van Heeswijk is less interested in composing objects than in generating "involutions." The word might sound somewhat strange. I use it in the meaning developed by Stephen Fuchs, in a chapter of a book called ***Against Essentialism***, where it is a question of "modes of association."[7] The primal mode of social association, social association at its level of greatest generality, writes Fuchs, is found in networks that tie together the meetings of persons in space and time, their communications and interactions. "Networks come first" (191). From them,

7. Stephan Fuchs. ***Against Essentialism*** (Cambridge: Harvard University Press, 2001). Page references for quotations are given parenthetically in the text.

"encounters, groups, and organizations" are generated, which should be considered as "variable and temporary 'involutions' or condensations of networks." These are a little like "eddies in rivers. They emerge as certain segments and clusters of a network turn inward, separating themselves to some degree from the overall structure and from the rest of the world" (192).

"Draw a line," "create an eddy": the two operations are parallel (and the chain continues in *Face Your World*). Again and again, what van Heeswijk has been doing for years is to offer all kinds of groups of people the means to "separat[e] themselves to some degree from the overall structure and from the rest of the world," in order to reduce the opening of a horizon that is, at the same time, the multiplication of possible worlds and the exteriority of total fragmentation. Because a practical necessity in the epoch of "super-differentiation" is to establish ways of reducing the overall openness, to establish nuclei of privacy for more than one individual, but nuclei which are not phobic. This is why the most common departure point for van Heeswijk's work is the definition of a membrane that provides for the relative enclosure of a portion of space and at the same time permits that space to communicate with its environment. Defining an envelope that allows an ephemeral and transitory community to separate itself from the overall structure and provide itself with its own time, while at the same time becoming the place for the projection of the images that actually generate this community: this, precisely, is the point where van Heeswijk's work begins.

Setting up a membrane and proposing a series of artifacts: the works begin in this way. Partially closing off a portion of space, opening this space to a particular collective, and providing the community in question with instruments that can be used to produce little universes, made up of parts of the world as it is, but recombined. Because it is around such universes that the encounters become denser. And the densification of a system of encounters, such that their images are multiplied, is what van Heeswijk is interested in producing.

The hybrid compositions of membranes, systems of

transportation, programs of action and multipliers of images that make up these works are meant less to anchor spaces of reserve within fixed territories, than to generate partially open interiorities, where it is possible for a community (no matter how transitory) to maintain itself in its own indetermination and at the same time, to multiply its links with a world that it continually approaches – and which supplies it with the materials that the mediations of the common can be made from – while at the same time responding to the demand that some production emerge from all this (an image, a text, a sequence of sounds), a production that can be presented to someone else.

Each time, it is a matter of provoking the involution of a network into a nest, but also, of ensuring the re-exportation of this nest into a network. For van Heeswijk, it is always a matter of defining a membrane that encloses and half-opens a space, it is a matter of producing a system to import individuals within the inner space of the membrane, then exporting the system that has thus been constituted. Constructing capsules, encapsulating

collectivities, transporting them elsewhere. Proposing images, giving them the means to be recomposed, laying out spaces for exhibition.

What discipline can van Heeswijk be said to practice? None that has an indubitable name or that structures itself in the way the disciplines did under the conditions of modernity. If it is worth maintaining the name of "art" to refer to these things, it is for convenience, and also because they share a relation of descent with the things that certain people have produced in the name of this venerable name, over the long course of modernity. At the same time, van Heeswijk's practice implies a strategic approximation and use of the institutions and territories that have arisen around the figure of modern art, and a reception of that which is most valuable in the artistic tradition: the belief that a certain practice of space, action, speech, and the image is capable of intervening in that which, from epoch to epoch, forms a central point where intense anxiety meets the source of all promises. But this same faithfulness requires her to propose, not objects structured in a certain manner (or gestures of simple rebellion against the paradigm of the object), but complex formations instead, agglutinations of elements and processes; and it also requires her to focus her interest less on the definitions of contents and forms that she has conceived in her solitude and reserve, than on proposals of spaces and instruments, transports and programs, which necessarily escape her control. For no one who wishes to remain faithful to the best of this tradition can deprive herself today of recognizing that we are dealing with an original situation: that of addressing ourselves to individuals who constitute themselves through the interanimation of observations, actions, and discourses, which they receive, simulate, and recombine (which they receive at the same time as they simulate and recombine them). Individuals who reach out in advance of what happens to them, with innumerable prosthetics and mediations, but at the same time find themselves exposed to new modes of fear and euphoria: to the fear that emerges in conditions where the modern forms of territorialization and integration dissolve, and to euphoria at the possibility of non-phobic territorializations and integrations.

This is why an artist who is fascinated by private faces in public spaces, breaks in dances, silences between things, and nests in networks, who assumes that the space of art should be occupied by attempts at connection, at the weaving of continuities and even of reparations, an artist who insists on defining membranes, on stabilizing and then projecting environments, finds herself faced, each time, with the need to take decisions for which almost nothing in the historical world that she inhabits can provide sufficient orientation. "Face Your World" also means this: situate yourself at that turning point where "moments could emerge which intervene with perception, so that new images or frameworks might come into being…" How is this done? The problem is deceivingly simple, and in truth, of extreme complexity. But what could be more necessary than posing the problem?

FACE YOUR WORLD

Reinaldo Laddaga is an assistant professor in the Department of Romance Languages at the University of Pennsylvania and author of the books *Baltasar Brum's Euphoria* (1999) and *Indigent Literatures and Base Pleasures* (2000), as well as many articles on issues of art and literature.

Translated from the Spanish by Brian Holmes.

SAWYER RECREA

GROUP PORTRAITS

The group portraiture of Holland could only develop its true form where each member of the group – while free to act autonomously – was nevertheless dedicated to the common good.
– Alois Riegl, *The Group Portraiture of Holland*

Public Art after Minimalism

Even a cursory stroll through a contemporary art exhibition reveals a salient fact about the situation of contemporary art: artists are no longer bound in principle or in practice to adhere to the norms and conventions of traditional art forms. For the last thirty years artists and critics have agreed (and continue to agree) that dispensing with the appurtenances of traditional painting and sculpture (ranging from the creation of the illusion of three dimensions on a flat surface, to hanging an object on a wall or putting it on a pedestal to be viewed) has opened up a new range of expressive possibilities for art and potential new experiences for viewers.

This idea can be traced back to the early years of the twentieth century with the emergence of the modernist avant-garde, but one more immediate source is the rise of minimalism in the United States in the mid 1960s. After performing a set of analytic and reductive operations on the work of art in an effort to determine what it was in essence, artists such as Robert Morris came to the conclusion that it was simply an object and that to experience it in its "truth" meant to experience it *in a situation*. Morris stated:

Robert Morris, *Untitled*, 1966
Plywood
48 x 96 x 96 inches (121.9 x 243.8 x 243.8 cm)
© 2002 Robert Morris / Artists Rights Society (ARS), New York

"The better new work [i.e., minimalism] takes relationships out of the work and makes them a function of space, light, and the viewer's field of vision. The object is but one of the terms in the newer aesthetic. It is in some way more reflexive, because one's awareness of oneself existing in the same space as the work is stronger than in previous work, with its many internal relationships. One is more aware than before that he himself is establishing relationships as he apprehends the object from various positions and under varying conditions of light and spatial context."[1]

Morris's approach made it clear that art making had outgrown its reliance on the norms of painting and sculpture as they had been passed down through history, and that it had entered a new phase – a kind of post-traditional condition – where the work of art could be inserted into the realm of everyday life and could be experienced within contexts like those that defined our daily commerce with the things of the world.

For the American artist Vito Acconci, the reduction of the work of art to an object in a situation drew attention to the framing function of the gallery/museum and provided further proof that traditional forms of art were no longer of any relevance to art making. Once inside the doors of an

art institution, he insisted, viewers were subjected to certain protocols of viewing and behaving. He stated, "when a person enters a gallery/museum, that person announces himself/herself as an art-viewer; the art-viewer submits to the terms of the art arena, the art viewer agrees to be a victim."[2] One of the "terms of the art arena" – the conditions under which art was to be experienced from within the confines of the gallery – was that the object be viewed from a distance, that it remain separated from the viewer in space, across the gap between the viewer and a painting on a wall or an object placed on a pedestal. For Acconci, the conditions under which we experience traditional works of art are socially and ideologically produced and preempt a meaningful encounter with art.

For this reason, Acconci began working outside the confines of the gallery/museum, and in doing so he helped establish new possibilities for public art. His work resonated with other artists who sought to inquire into the limitations of the

1. Robert Morris, *Continuous Project Altered Daily: The Writings of Robert Morris* (Cambridge: MIT Press, 1993), 15.

2. Vito Acconci, "Artist's Statements," in Linda Shearer, *Vito Acconci: Public Places* (New York: The Museum of Modern Art, 1988), 22.

institution of art and who also proposed alternatives in the form of art practices that engaged viewers in a direct and immediate way, free of the "terms of the art arena." Acconci stated, "public art, as a gathering place for people, functions as a model of the city" and "public art restores the peopled places that lead to discussions that lead to arguments that lead to reconsiderations that lead potentially to a revolution."[3]

Acconci's idea that public art should be a "gathering place for people" is made explicit in *Face of the Earth* (1984). Originally installed in an open, outdoor space, the work consisted of a series of five wooden platforms covered with Astroturf placed on top of each other and gradually stepped inward. The topmost platform contained four recessed openings with seats. The overall configuration of the piece, which was available to anyone standing on the ground or climbing to its top platform, was that of a human face. The four recessed openings on the top platform – its seats – created its eyes, nose, and mouth. Indeed, *Face of the Earth* was constructed like a kind of stage (a kind of "town square") on which people could assemble, free of the protocols of viewing they would be subjected to in a gallery or a museum.[4]

Face Your World

Dutch artist Jeanne van Heeswijk has stated that one of her goals has been to create works in which the static relationship between the viewer and the traditional work of art is overturned. Her aim has been to open up new possibilities of experience for viewers by creating works in which their role is active, not passive.

Vito Acconci, *Face of the Earth*, 1984
Astroturf covered wood
30 inches x 28 feet x 28 feet
(76.2 x 853.4 x 853.4 cm)
Photo courtesy of Acconci Studio

3. Ibid., 27.

4. Acconci made several versions of *Face of the Earth* between 1984 and 1988. In *Face of the Earth* 3 at Laumeier Sculpture Park in St. Louis (1988), the face is recessed into the ground instead of elevated above it and constructed of cement and sod instead of wood and Astroturf.

She said: "Visual art has always directed itself toward an audience – no audience, no art – but the motivations to turn the public into participants today is an entirely different question. A clear transformation from a static spectator to an active participant is at stake."[5] Like Acconci, van Heeswijk has sought to overcome the limitations inherent in the conventions and norms of traditional forms of art (such as painting) by creating works that institute a kind of public space, where viewers can come into direct contact with the work and each other.

Valley Vibes, *Demonstration*, 1998
Depford Market, London

Valley Vibes, *Valley Vibes Day*, 1999
Performances by Nico & Levy, local acoustic duo
Cafe at Oxford House, London

In a 1998 project in London titled *Valley Vibes* van Heeswijk (in collaboration with Amy Plant and CHORA – Institute for Architecture and Urbanism) fabricated a portable sound recording machine in the form of a large metallic box that looks like an ice cream trolley. It was to be used by the inhabitants of four inner-city neighborhoods in East London to broadcast information about the community, to stage events, and to serve as a kind of locally run recording studio. Called the "Vibe Detector," this machine has been instrumental in helping foster an indigenous inner-city culture and continues to be an integral part of the ongoing effort of the inhabitants to revitalize their community.

A similar process is at work in *Face Your World*. In this project van Heeswijk has once again brought her art into the public arena. With assistance from a multitude of collaborators, she has transformed a small commuter bus into a computer

5. Jeanne van Heeswijk, "Fleeting Images of Community" in Anette Balkema and Henk Slager, eds., "Exploding Aesthetics," *Lier en Boog* vol. 16 (Amsterdam, Atlanta: Rodopi, 2001), 178.

laboratory for children by retrofitting it with six high-tech computers and by installing custom built, ergonomically designed furniture.

The six computers on the bus house a computer program designed by van Heeswijk in collaboration with Maaike Engelen and V2_Lab. This program provided children with the opportunity to plan and build inner-city neighborhoods in a virtual world. The children's ideas and images were made available for public viewing at three community centers near downtown Columbus on computer monitors that were placed in large sculptures that also functioned as bus stops. The difference between van Heeswijk's computer program and commercial counterparts was that it allowed children to create visions of *their own* neighborhoods. The children generated photos of people, places, and things from their neighborhoods (using small digital "pen" cameras while traveling on the bus), and imported them into the program. They also were able to draw on a vast library of images from their surroundings that van Heeswijk (and Rolf Engelen) had supplied for them in advance.

Group Portraits

Yet *Face Your World* cannot simply be placed under the rubric of postminimalist public art. What makes *Face Your World* unique is the way it retrieves a past form of art and makes it relevant to the social conditions of the contemporary urban inner city.

This is revealed in the type of social interaction van Heeswijk has set up in *Face Your World*. The children who participate must do so *collectively*, and not just as individuals. The children are brought together as a group both on the bus and when they visit other neighborhoods, but more significantly when they are working on the computers. The computer program, which is called the Interactor, was set-up on a local area network (LAN) with multiuser capability. Each time one of the children entered the virtual world of the Interactor to begin designing a neighborhood, s/he encountered the other five players, who were present in the same virtual world. Any action undertaken by a child is an action that is fraught with potential consequences for the others. A child may decide to build a house on a plot of land that has been reserved by another child for a playground. At this point the avatar of the game, a virtual figure called Max Moore (named after an actual

person – Max A. Moore, Project Coordinator for Columbus Mayor Michael B. Coleman's Downtown Business Plan) enters the mix to broker a deal between the players.[6] Cooperation and civic responsibility establish the practical and ethical dimensions of the Interactor.

The emphasis on group activity in the Interactor is visually reinforced in the virtual world of the program. As the children wind their way through this world using the arrow keys on their keyboards, they run into virtual representations of each other. In these representations, they appear to each other in and through the mediating influence of a kind of colored "uniform"

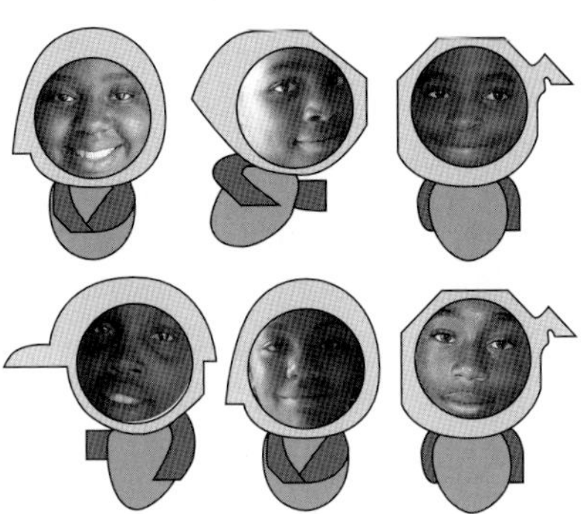

that contains an image of their face. This "uniform" gives the children a group identity and signals membership in a kind of civic collective. Group membership is also conferred on the children in the "real world," so to speak, by a log-on code (a secret password) that they are given in order to gain

6. The virtual figure of Max Moore also enters the game at certain points asking the children a series of open-ended questions to help them think about the different possibilities at their disposal for planning their neighborhoods.

access to the Interactor. This personal access code is each child's passport number, inscribed in the passport booklet that allows them to travel on the bus.

This conflation of strategies and details in *Face Your World* – an emphasis on collective activity and on peer identification through uniformity of appearance (and, in the case of the virtual figure of Max Moore, acceptance of a person of authority) – allows van Heeswijk to retrieve a past form of art. Donning their "uniforms" and carrying standards and banners that announce their presence and the ceremony of their endeavors (especially as they are shown on the graphical design covering the outside of the bus), the children who inhabit the virtual world of *Face Your World* are the latter day equivalents to the standard bearers and military officials who populate many Dutch

Cornelis Ketel, *Company of Captain Dirck Jacobsz. Rosecrans and Lieutenant Pauw, Amsterdam, 1588*, 1588
Oil on canvas
82 x 161 $^1/_2$ inches (208 x 410 cm)
Rijksmuseum, Amsterdam

Frans Hals, *Company of Captain Reinier Reael, known as the "Meagre Company,"* 1637
Oil on canvas
82 $^1/_4$ x 168 $^3/_4$ inches (209 x 429 cm)
Rijksmuseum, Amsterdam

group portrait paintings of the sixteenth and seventeenth century – in particular, the civic guard paintings by such artists as Cornelis Ketel, Frans Hals, and Rembrandt van Rijn. Indeed, the virtual figure of the urban planner Max Moore

Rembrandt van Rijn, *The Nightwatch*, 1642
Oil on canvas
142 $^7/_8$ x 172 inches (363 x 437 cm)
Rijksmuseum, Amsterdam

your help to find out how you want the world around you to be. Help me build your future world…Come on, let's face it!" Both Banning Cocq and Max Moore, in their respective material embodiments and through their verbal commands/gestures, mark the point at which a collective enterprise begins – mark the point around which a kind of corporate entity is formed and group activity is initiated.

is a kind of latter day virtual equivalent to Frans Banning Cocq, the central figure in Rembrandt's celebrated group portrait *The Nightwatch*. Cocq commands his company to "head out" with a forward gesture of his left hand. Moore leads the charge in the tutorial that opens the Interactor program with a command for the children to join him in the task of improving their neighborhoods and to take charge of their world. In this opening salvo, Max Moore says: "Building the world is what we do all the time. Now we need to build more than ever to change this city. We need to create more places to go to and hang out in…We work in a team all the time. I really need new team players. Maybe you have plans I never thought about. I need

These similarities only scratch the surface of the homology between *Face Your World* and sixteenth- and seventeenth-century Dutch group portrait painting. What makes *Face Your World* unique in its constellation of present and past cultural forms and practices is not simply how it recovers the motifs and presentational forms of the Dutch group portrait of the sixteenth and seventeenth centuries – its standard bearers, uniformed individuals, leaders, etc. – but the extent to which it recuperates its civic *ethos*, and how it translates this *ethos* from painting into site-specific project-based public art.

The clearest explanation of this *ethos* is found in the work of the German art historian Alois Riegl.

In his pioneering study of the Dutch group portrait, published in 1902, Riegl argued that Dutch painting, in particular group portraiture produced in the Netherlands between the fifteenth and seventeenth centuries, reflected the distinct outlook of the Dutch towards the world – what he called the Dutch **Kunstwollen**. For Riegl, the Dutch **Kunstwollen** was characterized by what he called "attentiveness." In his typology of psychological modes, "attentiveness" referred to an attitude towards the external world in which human beings sought neither to subordinate it to their wills nor to succumb to it. For Riegl, "attentiveness" indicates a mode of relation to the world and others that acknowledges simultaneously the mutual autonomy of the other and the willingness to engage with the other in a relation of reciprocity. Describing this state, he says: "The individual becomes open to the outside world, not in order to subjugate it, to unite with it in pleasure or to recoil from it in displeasure, but in pure, selfless interest. On the one hand, attentiveness is passive, since it allows external things to affect it without attempting to overcome them;

at the same time, it is active, since it searches things out, though without attempting to make them subservient to selfish pleasure."[7]

In Dutch group portrait painting Riegl argues that "attentiveness," as an attitude that speaks to a certain type of social relation between people, is communicated via a series of formal and aesthetic innovations. Included in these innovations is the ability to strike a compositional balance between individual identity and group activity. Nowhere in the fully achieved Dutch group portrait are individuals completely subordinated to or absorbed by a single governing action or figure, nor, however, does the concern with individuality overtake and subsume the interest in group action and corporate identity. In a discussion of Ketel's painting shown above, Riegl states: "Now the presentation motif [the motif where the leader is shown pointing out or presenting his second-in-command] is based on

7. Alois Riegl, *The Group Portraiture of Holland*, trans. Evelyn M. Kain (Los Angeles: Getty Research Institute for the History of Art and the Humanities, 1999), 75.

subordination, because the coherence of the whole [i.e., all the people depicted] revolves exclusively around the captain. On the other hand, the varied, self-assured poses of the figures reveal once again a tendency toward coordination, as they are obviously not under command but rather acting on their own private initiative."[8] In the Dutch group portrait the dialectical tension between part and whole – between individual and collective entity and activity – is momentarily reconciled, projecting an ideal of social cohesion that provides the basis for a democratic social order.

For Riegl this reconciliation is manifest not only in the internal relations of the painting (i.e., in the relations between the people depicted) but also in its external relations (in the relations between the depicted figures and the spectator/viewer). In a work such as Rembrandt's ***Syndics of the Cloth Guild***, the viewer is brought into direct and immediate contact with the depicted figures via a series of glances that are directed out of the space of the painting and into the space of the viewer. In the ***Syndics*** the viewer is addressed by the panel of merchants in the painting as an ***equal*** – as someone whose presence before the painting seems entirely appropriate and consequential. Rembrandt's painting exists in a state in which its outside (the viewer) and its inside (its depicted figures) are momentarily reconciled.

Face Your World recovers this ***ethos*** and the formal innovations associated with it by translating them into the Interactor. As we have seen, when children operate within the virtual world of the program, the relations they establish with the other players (the relations internal to the game) are conducted within the purview of "attentiveness" – with respect and cooperation. As the children work in the virtual world of the Interactor, designing and creating city

Rembrandt van Rijn,
Syndics of the Cloth Guild, 1661–2
Oil on canvas
75 $^3/_8$ x 109 $^7/_8$ inches (191.5 x 279 cm)
Rijksmuseum, Amsterdam

8. Ibid., 177.

neighborhoods, they are free to make individual decisions, but they must be aware of how their decisions may affect others and be prepared to enter into discussions with Max Moore and their peers to resolve disputes. As in the Dutch group portrait, individual identities are subordinated to, but not overwhelmed by, the imperative to act in concert.

Likewise, external relations – the relations between the players and the program itself – are founded on a similar acknowledgment of reciprocity. Max Moore's cry to take up the cause of urban revitalization in his introductory tutorial is a verbal equivalent to the glances of the Syndics in Rembrandt's painting, which are directed toward the viewer.

Thus, in *Face Your World* van Heeswijk has found a way to address the demand and need for civic identity and collective agency in the contemporary inner city in much the same manner that Riegl suggested Ketel, Hals, and Rembrandt did in seventeenth-century Amsterdam and Haarlem. To see *Face Your World* as an exercise in the construction and propagation of civic identities is

to understand something about how it embodies a similar desire to give rise to and express a latent democratic spirit in inner-city neighborhoods in Columbus. Van Heeswijk's mobilization of public space in *Face Your World* does so with a view to how it can be used to reclaim or retrieve the cultural forms of the past and the meanings they carried and how they can be recontextualized in the present. For van Heeswijk, the past is not a repository of cultural forms that are no longer relevant to the present, but a set of possibilities to be realized now.

This idea – that the cultural forms of the past are possibilities to be realized in the present – is an index of the different sensibilities of *Face Your World* and some other works of public art, such as Acconci's *Face of the Earth*. In *Face Your World* the retrieval of a past form of art is not the product of antiquarian interest but of awareness that historical forms are constitutive of our attempts to come to terms with and understand our present and not something that can be overcome or dispensed with altogether. It is an acknowledgment that history is, as the German philosopher Hans Georg Gadamer has said, "effective" – that consciousness (of the present) is situated in a web of historical effects that determine its shape as much as it determines them.[9] In *Face Your World* the historical past is not something over and done with but the very medium in which we think and act.

Acconci's desire to create a public art of free and open spaces uncorrupted by historically produced protocols of viewing cannot escape its own implication in history – cannot escape the potential of effective history to set the terms and conditions in which he understands his present. In *Face of the Earth*, for instance, his use of an anonymous face-image as the means to integrate a group of people in a single space – to bring them together in a realm of commonality – bears a resemblance to the image on the engraved title page of the first edition of Thomas Hobbes's *Leviathan*, where the citizens of a country find their common ground in the bodily image of a sovereign. By utilizing an image with a similar metaphorical thrust,

9. Hans-Georg Gadamer, *Truth and Method*, trans. Donald G. Marshall and Joel Weinsheimer (New York: Continuum, 1994), 300–07.

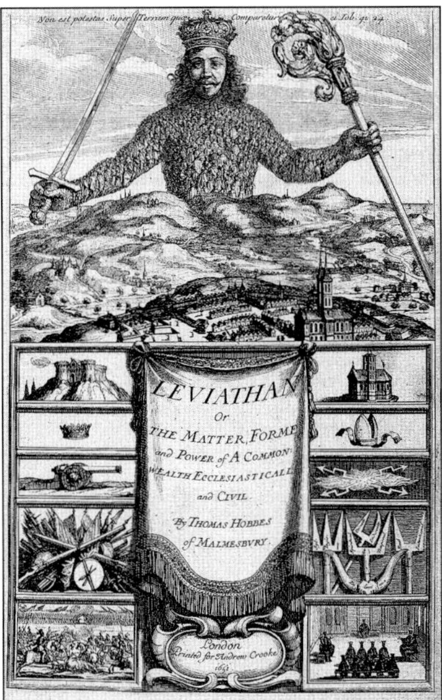

Title page illustration for Thomas Hobbes's *Leviathan*, first edition, 1651 (detail) Photo © The British Library, 522K6 F.P.

Acconci has, perhaps unwittingly, retrieved one of the presuppositions of seventeenth-century liberal political theory: that rule by an absolute monarch is a just form of government.

This unwitting retrieval of the past has also prevented Acconci from seeing the extent to which *Face of the Earth*, with its magisterial gaze, also provides a fitting visual equivalent to the Marxist philosopher Louis Althusser's explication of the function of ideology. In his characteristic torturous prose, Althusser stated: "The structure of all ideology, interpellating individuals as subjects in the name of a Unique and Absolute Subject is *speculary*, i.e., a mirror-structure, and *doubly* speculary: this mirror duplication is constitutive of ideology and ensures its functioning. Which means that all ideology is *centered*, that the Absolute Subject occupies the unique place of the Center, and inter-pellates around it the infinity of individuals into *subjects* in a double mirror-connection such that it subjects the subjects to the Subject, while giving them in the subject, in which each subject can contemplate its own image (present and future)…"[10] For Althusser, the function of ideology is to bring people to self-awareness by allowing them to recognize, in the impersonal image of an absolute and transcendent ego/subject (which could be an absolute ruler or any other figure of transcendent authority), a mirror image of themselves as autonomous, fully integral beings. This not only confirms their existence as social actors but insures the transcendence of the absolute subject as well.

In *Face of the Earth* collective identity is not achieved through the mutual interaction and reciprocity of its viewers/ participants; rather, it is conferred on them through identification with an external and impersonal authority. Thus, it is not the product of a voluntary association of autonomous individuals and is not an immanent dimension of their collective activity. The democratic possibilities of a form of public art such as this have, through an unreflective appropriation of history, given way to a type of sociality inappropriate for urban life in the twenty-first century.

Thus, there is a qualitative difference between the forms of sociality mobilized by Acconci in *Face of the Earth* and by van Heeswijk in *Face Your World*. In *Face Your World*, collective or corporate identity is achieved via the Interactor. The Interactor is the pretext in and through which its users could codiscover the nascent bonds of civic life. The children who participated in the project could become agents of social and cultural change insofar as they acknowledged the presence of

10. Louis Althusser, *Lenin and Philosophy and Other Essays* quoted in Alex Callinicos, *Althusser's Marxism* (London, Pluto Press, 1978), 66.

the other participants as agents of social and cultural change as well. Thus, in *Face Your World* the momentary reconciliation between individual desire and group priorities gave rise to a collective enterprise, or as Riegl stated, an association of autonomous individuals who have come together into a collective body for a "specific, shared, practical, and public-spirited purpose."[11]

What is at stake, therefore, in projects such as *Face Your World*, is how past forms of art can shape our attempts to make sense of the present and how and in what way(s) these forms of art can establish models for genuinely new and desirable social forms and patterns of interaction. Thus, to make a judgment about the success of *Face Your World* – a judgment about its success in engendering a new and desirable social form – is also to make a judgment about its success *as a work of art*. Van Heeswijk's retrieval of the Dutch *Kunstwollen* – her retrieval of "attentiveness" – is a retrieval of the ethical dimensions of Dutch group portrait painting of the sixteenth and seventeenth centuries.

For van Heeswijk, questions about the quality of our social relations are indissolubly connected to questions about art – about how the presentational forms of traditional art (in this case Dutch group portrait painting) can help us formulate the terms of negotiation with our present situation.

11. Alois Riegl, *The Group Portraiture of Holland*, 62.

Steven Hunt is co-curator of *Face Your World*. He is a graduate associate at the Wexner Center for the Arts and a doctoral student in the Department of History of Art at The Ohio State University.

STOP
CLEVELAND
THE JOB
OF THE ARTIST
IS ALWAYS
DEEPEN THE
MYSTERY

THE WORLD ACCORDING TO THE INTERACTOR: A LETTER

0. Interaction versus Transaction

Constant revolutionizing of production, uninterrupted disturbance of all social conditions, everlasting uncertainty and agitation distinguish the bourgeois epoch from all earlier ones. All fixed, fast frozen relations, with their train of ancient and venerable prejudices and opinions, are swept away, all new-formed ones become antiquated before they can ossify. All that is solid melts into air, all that is holy is profaned, and man is at last compelled to face with sober senses his real condition of life and his relations with his kind.
– *The Communist Manifesto*

The capitalistic mode of thought[1] produces subjects as actors. The actor can't exist alone. It needs others, but only to negotiate about the needs it has as a subject. The basis of living together is negotiation in order to survive. This leads to a manipulative attitude towards life in general and education in specific. The subject will never find any rest in being together; it always has to take into account the demand from others to negotiate. So being together is, fundamentally, a struggle. This way of dealing with each other can be characterized by the notion of *transaction*.

On the other hand, the *interactive* way of dealing with each other also presupposes the necessity of togetherness, but it lacks the demand for negotiation. In fact, questions about how we live together and what we mean to each other are not asked, because life is understood as *togetherness for its own sake*. Being together itself is the value of life and not the product one can reach by working together.

1. I will use "the capitalistic mode of thought" as referring to the conglomerate of ethical, anthropological, and ontological ideas and attitudes often associated with capitalism as defined in the Marxist and neo-Marxist intellectual traditions. Capitalistic societies are those societies whose institutions are based on, and facilitate, free enterprise and the production of (financial) value growth.

The little daydreamer who has this attitude is because of it not so keen on negotiating with other children, not so keen on being social or political or manipulative. The little daydreamer finds it enough to act as he or she feels and finds this natural in others as well. So the little daydreamer's starting point is feeling peaceful in just being together and doing as one thinks necessary in the specific situation. Because of his or her attitude, working together is a choice and not a need: it is free and not a requirement, it is friendly and not competitive. It is based on giving every single person the chance to develop him- or herself, and not based on trying to be the best one of all. This attitude is free and not competitive because, in it, one is *together* anyway from the start, whereas in the capitalistic mode of thought one is *related* from the start.

The Interactor tries to stimulate this interactive way of thinking, which the program's creators think is discouraged in most educational systems. They believe that much gets killed in most educational systems. Educational systems in this day and age favor transaction over interaction and so encourage children to be competitive and good negotiators: they are educating to create the best manipulator.

Some schools are aware of this problem and try to develop educational approaches to address it. A number of school types arose out of the wish to respect togetherness: Montessori schools, Waldorf schools, the Dalton and Jena Plan schools, and others. All of them try to educate a child because of the value that child has for its own sake. All seek to encourage the child to learn and develop on the basis of that specific child's personality and situation, not thinking about the use the education will have for society or others in the first place, but trusting this will become clear in time by itself.

But these types of educational systems easily lead to troubles for the child when it grows older. It then has to adapt one way or another to the "normal" way of being educated and has to answer one way or another to the demands society places. So it is not exceptional for children who were educated in one of these "free" ways to grow unhappy later in life because they feel the tension between the two ways of thinking every day in their own functioning. But in ordinary types of education people also think about how to prevent the capitalistic mode of thought from taking over completely. In the Netherlands, for instance, philosophy is now part of the regular curriculum of a vocational school for the first time.[2] The idea is to help children become more self-reflective by encouraging them to think independently and critically, not along the lines of any socially desired form of correctness. To show them what it means to only follow the paths of thinking itself, in the hope that they will discover the beauty and truth in thinking for the sake of thinking only, instead of seeing thinking only as a tool with which to discover solutions for problems.

The Interactor is aware of this issue as well. It does not resolve it, but it tries to help educators, and those being educated, find a way in which both types of thinking can be combined in a traditional educational system.

1. Introduction

In this letter I want to tell you how the Interactor can improve the idea children have about their influence over their environment. Let me first tell you how the Interactor works. It is a game that has to be played by six children at the same time. It is impossible to play it by yourself. The children together build the world they want, using pictures they take themselves and materials from the "library" of the Interactor, which contains over five hundred digital images taken in the neighborhoods where the children live.

2. I introduced philosophy as a subject in the vocational section of Thomas More College in The Hague. The practical challenge of how to deal with the problems this school has because of the tension between *relatedness* and *togetherness* as pointed out in this letter, and the ideas and expectations on how to improve this situation as they are being developed by the principal of the school, helped me to think about the meaning of the Interactor in specific and the ideas behind it in general.

They start building in a private space but very soon they bump into each other and have to talk with each other to determine whether or not they are allowed to build in someone else's area. Around these private spaces is a free space where all the kids can build together as they like, but here also there are some rules. For instance, they are not allowed to destroy each other's work by putting things on top of each other.

The Interactor is personalized by featuring a city planner character named Max Moore as a guide. (The character is named after a real city planner in Columbus, Ohio. Max Moore is project coordinator for the Downtown Business Plan of the City of Columbus.) Every ten minutes he asks the children a question about what they are doing. The questions are meant to help the children think about what they are doing in a constructive way. The answers the children give have no consequences for their activities unless they choose this themselves. The questions are suggestions about how to build a world that is nice to live in, but they also encourage the children to think about their environment in a reflective way. In playing the game, the experiences of the ***freedom to change the world*** and the ***connectedness of individuals in society*** emerge as each requiring and reinforcing the other. In what follows I will explain that these two angles are necessary to foster a reflective and critical attitude in children.

2. Reflection

The main thought behind the Interactor is to encourage children to become aware of their environment and their relations with it. When children come to reflect on themselves and their wishes in relation to their actions, they will see that their deeds can make a difference, not just in the game, but also in the real world. They are encouraged to not take the world as it appears for granted, to not believe that it is beyond their influence. To change the world by starting changing yourself, so to speak. This is an old thought and very much a cliché, but in a typical educational situation the "change it yourself" is often understood as "be a good child and listen to the wishes and commands of adults." Children are rarely encouraged to find out for themselves what they want and think, why they want and think it, and how their wishes and thoughts can, or could, influence their environment.

For the Interactor, children are little thinkers. But they also need guidance. So the adult is seen more as a guide than as a moral ruler who has to teach the children good behavior. That is why the city planner in the Interactor only asks questions and is not prescriptive about what would be a "good world to live in."

The children could create a gloomy world if they decide that together. They could create a violent world if they decide that together. They also could create a world impossible to live in, again if they decide that together. But along their way toward their world, they will be asked questions that will make them think about what they are doing; they will have to make choices consciously.

The nature of the exchanges between the children about how to build their world is kept as open as possible. Aside from a time limit for reaching a decision, they are free in how they deal – transact or interact – with each other. Here, too, the underlying thought is to give the children as much responsibility as possible and no more instruction than necessary. From an educational point of view, it might be said that the children are encouraged in this way to make their decisions their way. The thought is that because they are building together they will find out soon enough what will and won't work through their conversations with each other.

So the essential element in the game is the fact that the players have to work together. It is impossible to play the Interactor game alone. This is a prescriptive part of the game. It is intended to keep the children from thinking or feeling that the world is something that can be built in isolation. In this game the actions of any one child count as much as those of any other. In the real world this is not the case. Some actions are seen to be much more important than others. The higher someone's place in a hierarchy, the more important that person is to the world, to put it bluntly. Young children are implicitly encouraged to think about themselves and their actions in this hierarchical way. Many do not think that way at first. They soon acquire this attitude, however, because of how educational systems work. They have to achieve and compete to become noticed as someone of importance in the world.

As a result of this way of raising and educating children, in later life many people feel confused about their ability to influence the world. They wonder: What value is there in having a little job in a nowhere place? Does that count in the world? Does it make a difference in our world? Does it matter how I act in this job? Or in our world? Do I contribute to our world? Whatever may be the case, people have to stay competitive and have to keep achieving, even to defend a little job – so they learn to act as politely as possible to keep at least what they have.

There is a double-edge in educating children to be polite and well behaved. It is difficult for a child to stay in touch with the feeling that these things are valuable for their own sake and not only for what you can get for them (hopefully as much as possible). They lose the deeper feeling that in every action one makes a real difference in our world. Seen from that perspective, there are no little jobs or more important ones, only work that has to be done or fun that people want to have together, or beauty that one needs to create out of the value of beauty itself. On the other hand, it is impossible to raise children without awareness of the need for competition, for they have no chance whatsoever without it. This is a tension in educational systems all over the world, and teachers are, in many cases, well aware of it. How to deal with this tension is the question to think about, and one way to answer it is to take children more seriously in their own being, as the Interactor tries to do.

3. Education

But what am I saying? What does it mean to take children seriously in their own being? They need to be raised, and they do not always do what is good for them, or rather they often want what is not that good for them. Educational thinking favors "threats"; the moment the child is not behaving as expected, threats come in: "no cookies today," "no playground today," or whatever the parent, or later, the teacher, knows the child doesn't want to miss. Cruel parents are very skilled in inventing horrible punishments for their children, and so are cruel teachers. Nobody likes that kind of punishment, but what about "threats" in general? The general threat of not becoming an important adult? Not becoming a worthwhile part of society? Many people use that threat without even thinking about it: If you do not work well at school, what about your future? You must have good grades, never mind if you like a subject or not, or find it useful at this moment in your life, or have something else on your mind. No matter what, get your good grades, because they really count: the better your grades are, the better your next school can be.

But what about the wondering child, the child with stars in the eyes and a heart of gold, the child walking through life simply loving the wind and a rainy day? What about all the little dreamers among us, all the little lazy, playful, good-natured late bloomers, all the sweet, not-at-all-competitive children, all the children who have a real interest at a very young age? What about all these different kinds of children, of people? Is there an educational system for them, which makes them really grow? I do not think so. These children are punished by the threats of parents and society: "You will not amount to anything!" Some of these children are lucky because they are talented and their talent will help them out, but all those without the gift of a talent, what about them? They will become the adults with a lot of anger deep in their hearts, about society and life in general. Their dreams, their plans, their good hearts, their noncompetitive natures, their friendly spirits – when all of those have been subsumed into the economic system, but with little financial return, people do not feel too good about what they do. They will raise their children with the same spirit of anger or revenge, and so on and so on. And the only answer society has to this problem is to consume even more or to propagate a strict, often fundamentalist, institutionalized religion or morality. Neither is free at all.

What does freedom mean from an educational point of view? Freedom in pedagogy doesn't mean: go ahead, do as you like, go where you want, read what you please, learn only what you want to learn, and everything will turn out fine. No, that has been tried!

4. Stimulation

But what does a computer game have to do with all this? Family games we all know. They are supposed to be enjoyable for the family, letting them be together and have a good time. But most games are based on having a winner – and it can take a while before a child can bear the fact it is possible to lose the game. The winner did best, and the loser didn't play that well. For very ambitious children, family games are often less than pleasant: they become so focused on winning that they do not see the fun of the game anymore. Adults say, "It doesn't matter if you lose or win, what's important is to have fun." The child knows better…Yes, it is only a game, but we play games all our lives, and some day it turns out that the game has become so serious it is impossible to say it's only a game. You simply have lost, and you find yourself not where you wanted to be from the start.

"Winning the game," isn't that a proper characterization of the capitalist mode of thought that I have been talking about? The reason behind this is that capitalist societies see the individual as the center of the world. A center, island, or atom that has to decide by itself if it will deal or not deal with others – that is how freedom presents itself in most societies today. This freedom is fundamentally negotiation.

"Negotiation." When I want something, I will have to try to get it. That is quite a different way of being in the world than the perspective in which we are all connected and need each other to be free from the start in a completely equal way. In that perspective, nobody will try to use somebody else to get what he or she wants. This is of course a highly idealistic way of thinking, and in daily life it often doesn't work that way at all. Friendship, animosity, politics, strategies, all thoughts about how to get what one wants in life, even the most simple practice of striving to be morally good, are factors in a process of producing winners, because the person employing them expects to get something out of that practice.

Children growing up start negotiating as well and lose their initial attitude of doing well by others and themselves without asking for favors in return. Children start out setting the right example, but most depart from it before they're ten years old. In contemporary societies children more and more represent the impossibilities of the system. Despite the rhetoric and regulations that we develop to give children a central and safe place in our world, there seems to be less and less room for children to be themselves. Every parent feels in a child the hope for a future not bound to this limited way of living, and every parent contributes to the loss of that hope for the child and in the child.

Contradictorily enough it is capitalism itself, connected with the religious systems belonging to it, which provided the mental space in which the thought could arise against itself. After the modern era in philosophy had discredited the notion of intrinsic value, and with that the notion of final causality, philosophers including David Hume, William James, Alfred North Whitehead, Gilles Deleuze, and Ernst Bloch, all in their own way made it very clear that life has meaning only when it is lived for its own sake and not for the rewards it may give. These philosophers all tried to add to traditional metaphysical thinking (which had not been able to provide a counterweight to the "transactionalization" of life), a new aspect, the aspect of the intrinsic connection of what is not realized, the possible, with what is already realized in the world. For these philosophers, every single element of life, from a stone to a human being, bears the openness of paradise (an orientation towards an ultimate openness that does not end – in Goethe's words, "the infinity native to all things") in every action it takes. It is not clear what this paradise will be, but it is clear that the openness to it in every single element of life not only connects all these elements together (it is what they all have in common and what they can feel in each other – their identity lies in the realm of possibility rather than in a ground that is already realized), it also makes them strive after beauty, harmony, and truth, although all of these have to be redefined from moment to moment. There is a pragmatic moment in the way truth is present in our lives. The infinity in things, the presence of what is possible, realizes itself as the opening up of what can be realized in the present context. Bloch called this ***concrete utopia***, in contrast to abstract or idealist utopias, such as those of early socialism, communism, and today, neo-liberalism.[3] In this sense, stripped from its reifying tendency, pragmatism is distinctly anti-capitalistic. The striving itself is a play of identity and difference and a struggle of opposites, but not a war of all against all.[4] By discovering the linkage between the concepts of novelty and possibility on the one hand and intrinsic value on the other, these philosophers have found a way out of the deadlock of capitalism. The profanation of all that is holy (***The Communist Manifesto***) can be countered, not by returning to a form of holiness that was before, but by moving beyond the logic of capitalism.

3. There are distinctly utopian elements in the discussions around globalization. We need only mention the works of Francis Fukuyama. For a discussion of the ethical dimensions specifically, see Hans Küng, ***A Global Ethic for Global Politics and Economics*** (New York: Oxford University Press, 1998).

4. The thoughts of Dutch philosopher Johan Siebers about Alfred North Whitehead and Ernst Bloch helped me a great deal in formulating this point of view. See Johan Siebers, ***The Method of Speculative Philosophy***, Dissertation, Leiden, 1998 (Kassel: Kassel University Press, 2002).

Now, let us go back to the Interactor and repeat the question raised earlier: what does a computer program have to do with these highly speculative thoughts? The desire to design a program like this arises out of the wish to contribute to a better world, a world in which every action of every human being counts and counts sufficiently to be able to change the world – as long as it is understood that an action cannot take place without the involvement of others. In life itself, togetherness is basic. In conscious life there is a tendency to lose contact with this basis, and objectify and externalize those aspects of life from which consciousness arises – aspects like myself, others, desires, ways of meeting my needs. That tendency is what I have called capitalism. Reappropriating togetherness consciously is what is so hard to do and what makes us human, at the same time. The effort is as much practice as it is theory: the Interactor, a practice (a game)[5] containing the theory, affords room for this effort.

The Interactor is designed so that children working with it are encouraged to understand their own interactions with their world. In educational systems one is rarely encouraged to reflect on one's own thoughts about life in general. One is encouraged instead to develop the intellectual and moral "skills" necessary to become a valuable part of society. Of course this is needed as well, but it loses its meaning after a while if children do not understand its meaning apart from simply fulfilling expectations. One can only deal with life in a responsible, careful, and caring way, if one has reflected on life in general and on one's own needs in general. It is not

5. A lot could be said about the relation between games and the thoughts I am talking about here. There are reasons for thinking that playing is central to the development of the awareness of togetherness, and recent ethological research indicates that animal play is a factor in the emergence of morality. I will not explore this topic here, however.

at all necessary to reach a point where it becomes clear what life in general means,[6] or who this person is in the deepest sense, but the course of reflection itself keeps alive the openness to hope for the fulfillment of beauty, harmony, and truth in the way described by the philosophers I mentioned before. Thinking about life in general does not lose itself in abstract, cloudy speculation; it is what is needed to be able to see the possibilities right in front of you, to be able to be open to concrete utopia.

The Interactor tries to stimulate this kind of thinking and this kind of feeling about oneself, others, and life in general, but it also gives insight into the difficulties such ways of thinking and feeling bring. What if a child is building a world with another child who is sabotaging actions all the time, is nasty, and doesn't want to cooperate? What to do about that? One has to talk, but after a while if the talk doesn't work, the city planner will decide for the children, and so the nasty one is overruled by the city planner's "better" point of view of building together. The children can't go on talking and talking all of the time, and they can't ruin the work someone else did. It is impossible to do that, because the program is designed to prevent it. An individual child can make a horrible place in the free space or prevent others from building in the free space completely so it can isolate itself during the building, but that means probably the others will also not give permission to build in their spaces as well, and so the isolation of the child will grow and the possibility of building will soon vanish. Of course that child also can decide to build its own place over and over again by deleting what it created

6. Far from it. The idea that, when we reflect and philosophize, we go for the "answer" to the question of "the meaning of life" is precisely the capitalist revenge at philosophy, its attempt to trivialize and humiliate reflective awareness, making fun of it, in the name of wisdom if need be. Just think of all the cultural products, books, films, etc., sincere or ironic, about "the meaning of life" – all of them encouraging subservient intellectual suicide and installing a taboo on philosophy, sometimes even under its guise. The murder of Socrates has become a continuously available industrial product, a *service*.

and starting again, over and over again. But is that much fun? In the Interactor the enticement to build together – the necessity of building together – is pretty strong. And so the child who wants to rule the world will have a hard time, and most likely will not like the game very much. This introduces a kind of tension that recalls the ideas of another philosopher, Bernard Mandeville, who believed that the vices of the individual (striving only for one's own good) lead to the virtues of society (the good of everyone). One could call this a typical capitalist thought, but one that has turned out to work pretty well. And our little pretty individualistic child could live very well with it.[7]

So the tension in the Interactor lies in the attempt to combine thoughts like this one of Mandeville's with those of such philosophers as Bloch. Both ways of thinking have their value in daily life. And the Interactor could not have been created if it had not acknowledged both of these thoughts. It is impossible to trust completely the deep wish children have for a beautiful, harmonious world in which people treat each other with complete honesty (the moment of truth), so the city planner is needed to guide the children and to prevent them from doing things to each other that could lead to a permanent state of war, of all against all. By seeking to prevent that from happening, we also address the thought that perhaps children are not so connected with each other after all. The disconnection arises with awareness of individual desires and wishes and has to be overcome in another kind of awareness. This is the purpose of education. The thought that people by nature desire harmony, beauty, and truth is as true as the thought that life is a constant struggle and competition between islands that mostly want to satisfy their own desires first.

7. In his ***Fable of the Bees***, subtitled "private vices, publick benefits" (1705), Mandeville recounts how evil vices such as luxury, greed, and envy all lead to public benefits by encouraging enterprise:

The Root of evil, Avarice,
That damn'd ill-natur'd baneful Vice,
Was Slave to Prodigality,
That Noble Sin; whilst Luxury
Employ'd a Million of the Poor,
And odious Pride a Million more.
Envy itself, and Vanity
Were Ministers of Industry.

5. Aspiration

The Interactor as a work of art expresses the problems and tensions I have been talking about. The expression takes place at the practical level, the theme has a general reach. The artist does not give "the solution" but she gives the problems a form and content in this game, and her hope is that the children working with it will become sensitive to the guiding thought at a concrete level. From the moment that they start to reflect on their own behavior and their wishes concerning their lives and their world, they will no longer be able to react only out of impulse. It is a challenge for the future to encourage children to be more self-reflective in general, to think for themselves in a way that is neither political nor moral but deeper and more critical, and to make their own decisions without being selfish or enslaved to ideologies, explicitly or implicitly. Yet this is a heavy demand on educational systems all over the world. It means asking them to take thinking seriously for its own sake, not for the use it has, or the career one can get from it. It means that all children, with whatever potential they are supposed to have, are encouraged to be thinkers – not just the very clever child or the child prodigy, but every single child, in every single school.

This will be almost impossible to realize in the near future, but adopting this approach toward children and what they need to learn changes, at a personal level, our interactions with children from the moment that reflection leads us to see the role and nature of thinking. And even if only one little child will find in this Interactor a stimulation for reflection, it will have done its work.

Maaike Engelen is a poet and philosopher who lives and works in Rotterdam. The author of **David Hume, hand in hand**, she is currently involved in developing a philosophy curriculum to be used in vocational schools in the Netherlands.

Aminah Brenda Lynn Robinson, *A Street Called Home*, 1997 (detail)
Mixed media
Columbus Museum of Art, Ohio: Museum Purchase with funds donated by Wolfe Associates, Inc.
© Aminah Brenda Lynn Robinson / Licensed by VAGA, New York.

VESTA A. H. DANIEL AND CYNTHIA COLLINS

COMMUNITY VISIONS

Children relate to their world in many different ways. They can and do use the information gained from daily experiences such as walking or riding to school, shopping, selecting what to eat and what to wear, and making choices about where they would like to go. They are not always aware that they are making choices, however, because many of these activities just seem necessary and routine. Moreover, some children do not know that choices are available to them. And, they do not always know that routine decisions can be connected to their world and their ongoing education, both in and out of school. The collaborative project *Face Your World*, initiated by artist Jeanne van Heeswijk, gave children the opportunity to identify the importance and power of making decisions. The project was a facilitator that provided children with a context for creating and exploring options that made them participants in shaping virtual worlds and, ideally, their real worlds as well.

The children participating in *Face Your World* create virtual worlds using the Interactor, the game-like computer program that is a central component of the project. Initially, it might seem that the children were just having a visual art experience that was fun and unusual. But they were also involved in working through a process sequentially; noticing and employing details; applying prior knowledge to a future vision; making choices based on contemplation and preference; being involved as individuals in a collaborative process; and identifying and addressing life-based issues. Other important aspects of the project involved interactions between art and technology, between information acquired through formal education and through "home knowledge" (what the children have learned from their experiences), and among a range of community participants (the children, instructors at the recreation centers, educators from the Wexner Center, guest speakers, etc.). Our interest in the project as educators was twofold: in the ways local communities, individuals, and environments became integral to the creative processes of *Face Your World* and in the implications the project might have for more formal learning contexts.

The children in this project were a community of artists charged with the task of creating/improving virtual environments while also exploring and examining the real environment of the city in which they live. This was their individual and collective mission. But the children were not the only community members actively engaged in *Face Your World*. The essay by Maaike Engelen elsewhere in this volume emphasizes the interactive contacts between children using the Interactor. Here the focus is instead on other kinds of interaction that shaped the project for both the artist and the participating children. In much of her work, van Heeswijk evidences strong interests in issues of location and the relationship between art and community. Related themes and ideas link the projects she has developed in varied European and U.S. locales, yet specifics often emerge from her perceptions of the communities in which her projects will take place. In preparation for *Face Your World*, she traveled to Columbus to visit the Wexner Center and the three recreation centers that became hosts for the project: Blackburn Recreation Center and Sawyer Recreation Center on Columbus's Near East Side, and the Boys & Girls Clubs of Columbus Westside Unit on the Near West Side. She wished to learn more about the Children of the Future program that takes place at these centers, and she wanted to see the neighborhoods in which the centers are located. On subsequent visits van Heeswijk and Rolf Engelen took digital images of various places and elements in these communities; the pictures formed the 500-image library for the Interactor, setting the program in the specific neighborhoods where most of the participating children live.

Van Heeswijk was also interested in meeting members of the local community who were involved in working with children and who had ongoing ties to the neighborhoods. One of the people with whom she met was Baba Olugbala, a sculptor and community activist who lives near the two recreation centers on the Near East Side. His home functions as a gallery and community gathering spot where he works with children and adults on art activities and events. The neighborhood in which Olugbala lives has historically been one of the centers of Columbus's African American community. Recently, it has attracted many new inhabitants, drawn by the area's handsome historic homes available at prices substantially below those of comparable structures in other parts of the city. This process is displacing many people from the area. Meanwhile, a number of community residents, including Olugbala, are committed to improving conditions without relinquishing the neighborhood's identity. As an homage to the contributions of African Americans in this community, Olugbala has sought to change its name to African Village, a choice that parallels the names such as German Village and Italian Village that have been selected to reflect the cultural heritage of other historical neighborhoods in Columbus. (The area is currently most often known as "Olde Town East," a designation that signals historicism without acknowledging specific peoples' histories.) Olugbala's stories about his neighborhood and specifically about his attempts to change the neighborhood's name critically inspired van Heeswijk's vision of the *Face Your World* project, contributing to her ideas about the particular issues of urban development that the Interactor game and the project as a whole would address.

The participating children came to the project with certain knowledge about their communities. They could identify particular structures such as their homes, schools, stores, bus stops, churches, and parks. But they may have had little understanding of how and by whom these things were created. Moreover, they may never have considered the possibility that they could actually change or create something in their environment or that choosing to change or create one thing would have consequences for many future choices. Throughout the course of *Face Your World*, a carefully chosen schedule of guest speakers, field trips, and other presentations illuminated and complemented the creative processes the children explored with the Interactor. "Photo stops" – the places the bus stopped during its daily routes so that the children could take additional images to use in the Interactor and add to its library – were also a significant part of the project. Collectively, these activities and visits offered real world insights and reinforced the idea that in their neighborhoods and city, just like in the virtual world of the Interactor, people share space and work together.

One guest speaker, city planner David Efland, introduced the children to varied planning concepts with a role-playing game. The children took the roles of a mayor, a real estate developer, and a private citizen in constructing a city. All of the children had a chance to play all of the roles. They had to agree on the placement of roads and train tracks and the use of buildings for public and private purposes. Certain planners had privileges that could not be vetoed by others. As the children worked through their roles they became more aware of the ways decisions in both the real and virtual worlds dovetail. Several speakers and trips opened up discussions of services essential in any large city. The children met with representatives from Columbus's Division of Water and Traffic Management Center, heard about public transportation at the Central Ohio Transit Authority (COTA) bus facility, and visited the city's Police Impound Lot where towed cars are housed. These experiences were essential for the children's understanding that real people make a city by performing crucial, although usually invisible, tasks such as making water safe to use, controlling traffic signals, and creating efficient and safe ways to transport people. In all instances, the children had the chance to see how these functions had changed over time, how their lives were connected to these services, and to think about a critical question: What would you do if you had control over these services?

Other field trips and photo stops suggested varied possibilities for recreational and educational uses of space. The children visited the Columbus Zoo, Franklin Park Conservatory (a historic "glasshouse" green house in a large urban park), Dodge Skatepark (a park with a halfpipe and other equipment especially for skateboarders and skaters), and The Topiary Garden (a representation of Georges Seurat's ***A Sunday on La Grand Jatte*** as a topiary sculpture). These visits too introduced numerous questions: Why are there parks or places like zoos or conservatories or works of public art? Who decides what kind of parks (or art) to put in a community?

The concept of history can be especially elusive to young children, so trips included historical as well as contemporary sites, and discussions often focused on how places (and perceptions of places) change over time. On a trip to Franklinton Cemetery, which dates back to 1799, the children saw memorial statues and grave markers that document the history of Franklinton, the oldest part of Columbus. The Boys and Girls Clubs Westside Unit is located in this Near West Side neighborhood. A topic of discussion at the cemetery was how and why cemeteries, once central environments in peoples' daily lives, are much less familiar to most children today. The children also visited German Village, a neighborhood built by German immigrants that is now one of Columbus's best-preserved and most affluent urban areas. They heard about the history of the community and the role historic preservation played in its transformation from a relatively poor area to a very prosperous one. They also were able to think about how that transformation may have affected residents, including those unable to afford to stay in what had been their community.

Understanding the past as a prerequisite for planning the future became a critical component of the children's experiences in *Face Your World*. By looking at the past, the children learned that communities are not static and that changes occur as a result of decisions made by individuals and groups. This might be new knowledge. By gathering information about how their communities were created and about how problems came into being and have been addressed, they gained understanding of how decisions impact their current and future existence.

Artist Aminah Brenda Lynn Robinson served as the children's guide in looking at the history of changes in one community familiar to many of them, the area around Mount Vernon

Avenue on the Near East Side of Columbus not far from Sawyer and Blackburn Recreation Centers. Robinson's work encompasses mixed-media paintings, sculptures, and illustrated books. Her presentation was based on her book *A Street Called Home*, which tells of life along Mount Vernon Avenue in the 1940s. Then the street was the central thoroughfare of a predominately African American neighborhood where Poindexter Village, the first public housing project in Columbus, was built. As a life-long resident and griot of Poindexter Village, Robinson has spent many hours investigating the history and memories of this community and of the neighborhood called the Blackberry Patch that became the site of Poindexter Village. She describes the Mount Vernon Avenue of the past as the heart of Poindexter Village, a bustling street boasting many small businesses, an open marketplace, and varied cultural activities. Then, because the area was isolated by freeways that cut it off physically and economically from the rest of the city, businesses struggled and many buildings were boarded up and abandoned. Today, residents and a few growing cultural institutions are working to revitalize the area.

A consummate storyteller, Robinson began her presentation by asking the children if they were at all familiar with Poindexter Village or the Blackberry Patch. There was no response from the audience, even through about two-thirds of the children live in that area. Robinson continued: "The destruction of the Blackberry Patch was necessary for the building and construction of Poindexter Village. The residents of the Blackberry Patch were African Americans who migrated from the South at the turn of the twentieth century. The residents of the Blackberry Patch were scattered all over the city. Poindexter Village is historically significant because it is the third major housing development built by the Metropolitan Housing Authority in the United States between 1939 and 1940. My parents were among the first residents in this new community." The artist then used her work to tell the children about their neighborhood, showing them how she portrays and interprets places like those depicted in the Interactor.

Robinson hopes that her presentation "inspired the young people to begin to talk to their elders about the community and to see the community with different eyes." Certainly her discussion opened up many questions: Why do places change? How can we make things change? How are some of the people from Poindexter Village connected to me? What do I want my community to look like in the future?

In *Face Your World*, van Heeswijk provided a space where voices such as Robinson's could speak and be heard. The specific and particularly local dimension this gives to the project is crucial in opening its creative space and processes to the participating children. One implication the project might have for educators is reinforcing or heightening awareness of how such immediate, local dimensions can invigorate educational situations. Other implications involve the collaborative and inquiry-based interactions stimulated by the Interactor software and the possibilities for broader community interaction nascent in the project.

Certainly, the children's experiences with the Interactor and the process of creating environments could be applicable beyond this project, including in schools. There too, its inquiry-based process for generating ideas could be applied to neighborhood and urban issues, with teachers and students asking such questions as "What places in your neighborhood do you like the most, and why? What things about your neighborhood would you like to change, and why? How would you go about making these changes?" As in the Interactor, the questions and answers can be built on one another. For example, an answer to the first question might be: "A place that I like in my neighborhood is the park, because many children can be there at the same time while their parents and grandparents wait for them on the benches in the shade. But, the park is not near my house, so I can't go there as much as I would like." After hearing about the work of a city planner, a child might then be asked: "If you were a city planner, how would you plan for parks?" A possible answer might be: "I would make sure that all of the neighborhoods have their own small parks with playgrounds for the children and shade trees and benches for the parents and grandparents. The city should make sure that there are lights for safety and water fountains. Right now, there are plenty of empty lots with weeds and rocks on them that nobody is using."

Face Your World was about possibilities. The children had the opportunity to be authors of their virtual worlds and to envision themselves as builders, planners, and collaborators. By assuming an active role in a constructive process, they could see connections between their lived experiences, their existing knowledge, new experiences, and ultimately new knowledge. As a final step in our discussion of *Face Your World*, let us speculate about extending another possibility suggested by the project.

An ongoing challenge for many children's programs, in and out of schools, is gaining the interest and participation of parents, neighbors, and other members of the community. In *Face Your World*, the installation of the bus stop kiosks outside of the three recreation centers was an important step toward such involvement. Each kiosk displayed various examples of the virtual worlds created by the children on a screen embedded in the sculptural form. The kiosks communicated that something interesting and different was going on in the community and enabled family, friends, and the children themselves to see their images in an intriguing, public context.

Doubtless many participating children also took the project "home," so to speak, in conversations with their parents, family, and friends. But how could the project seek out opportunities to be even more expansive in involving parents and other community members? What if it were truly convenient for parents and others to see what the children were doing on the bus? What if parents and neighborhood residents were invited to see how the project worked? Or even to participate themselves in processes developed as creatively as the Interactor? Because the recreation centers are "neutral spaces" in comparison to schools, possibilities for involving parents and others there might be particularly inviting. Neutral spaces allow people to be present in them without fear of being judged. In some schools, by contrast, parents can be intimated by the language used by educators. In the recreation centers, the atmosphere is more relaxed, allowing parents and children to feel free to participate at their own level of comfort.

Pondering the possibilities of approaches such as these extends *Face Your World*'s collaborative process of generating and sharing ideas. Thus, for educators and observers in the Columbus community, just as for participating children, the project continues as a source of ideas for future development.

Vesta A. H. Daniel is an associate professor in the Department of Art Education at The Ohio State University. Cynthia Collins is the educator for tours and community programs at the Wexner Center for the Arts, The Ohio State University.

A Guide to Face Your World

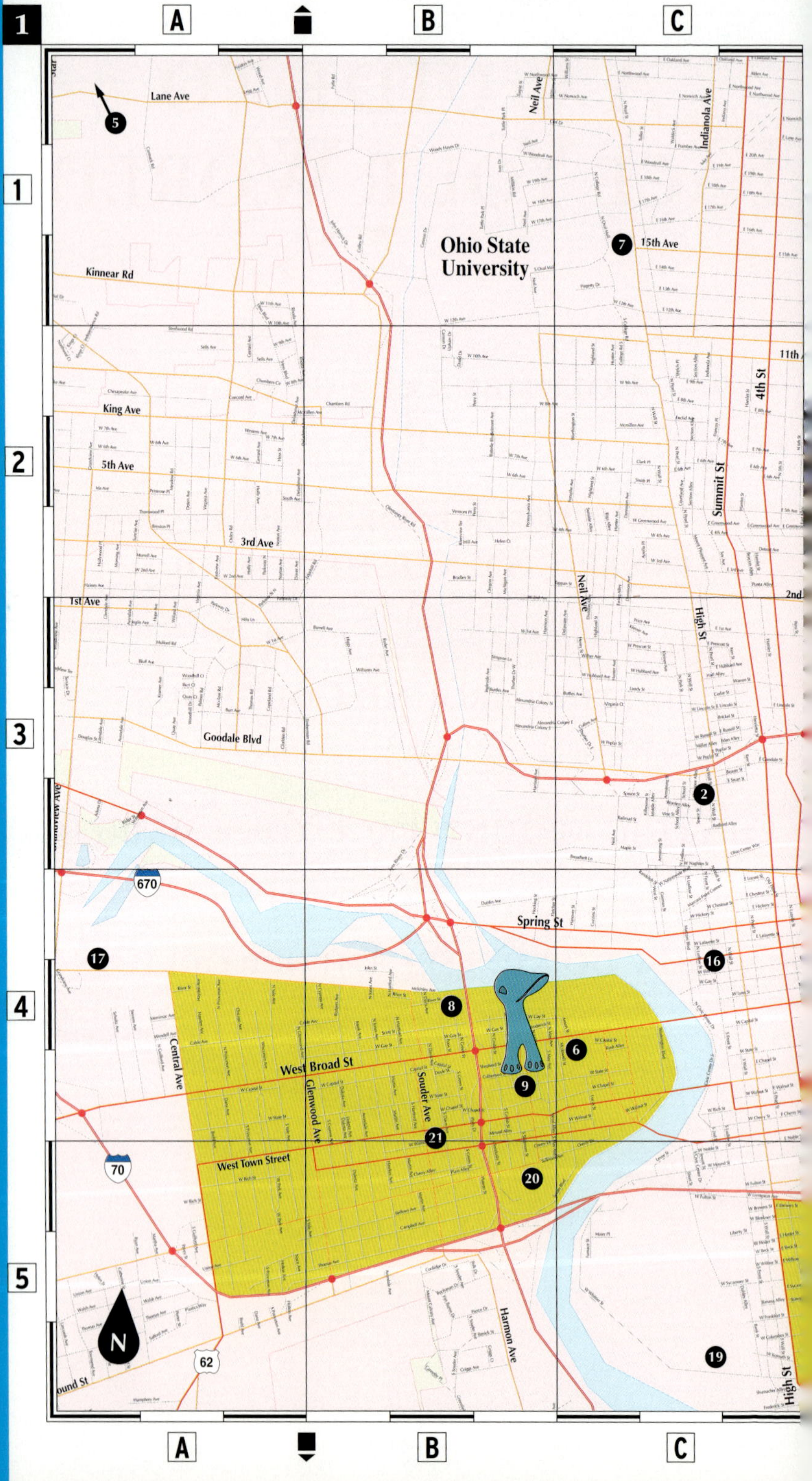
1
A
B
C
Lane Ave
Neil Ave
Indianola Ave
Ohio State University
15th Ave
Kinnear Rd
11th
4th St
King Ave
5th Ave
Summit St
3rd Ave
1st Ave
Neil Ave
High St
2nd
Goodale Blvd
670
Spring St
West Broad St
Central Ave
Glenwood Ave
Souder Ave
West Town Street
70
Harmon Ave
62
High St
1
2
3
4
5
5
7
2
17
16
8
6
9
21
20
19
N

D   E   F

2

1

German Village ①

North Market ②

Franklin Park Conservatory and Franklin Park ③

The Topiary Garden ④

Columbus Zoo ⑤

Toledo & Ohio Central Railroad Station ⑥

Wexner Center for the Arts ⑦

Franklinton Cemetery ⑧

Boys & Girls Clubs of Columbus Westside Unit ⑨

Poindexter Village ⑩

Mount Vernon Avenue ⑪

The King Arts Complex ⑫

Sawyer Recreation Center ⑬

Olde Town East or African Village ⑭

Blackburn Recreation Center ⑮

City of Columbus Traffic Management Center ⑯

Central Ohio Transit Authority (COTA) ⑰

Jim Arter's garden ⑱

City of Columbus Police Impound Lot ⑲

Dodge Skatepark ⑳

Franklinton Library ㉑

project site

photo stop

friday speaker

place on map

Columbus at a glance

Columbus, the capital of Ohio and the county seat of Franklin County, is the largest city in Ohio, the 15th largest in the United States, and among the fastest growing metropolitan areas in the northeast. Located in the center of the state, Columbus occupies an area of over 200 square miles. The diverse economy encompasses business, service, and manufacturing and is not reliant on one single industry. Sixteen colleges and universities are located in the area, including the main campus of The Ohio State University, the state's land grant university and, with over 48,000 students, one of the largest schools in the country. Major Columbus area employers include the state and federal governments, The Ohio State University, and automotive, banking, retail, and insurance corporations.

People and history

Over 1.5 million people live in the greater metropolitan area of Columbus. The population of Columbus itself, according to the 2000 census, is 711,470. Males make up 48.6% of the population; females 51.4%. Approximately 70% of the population is white, and 26% is black. Asians and Native Americans make up smaller percentages. Owner-occupied and renter-occupied housing is almost equally divided.

Among the earliest structures known to have occupied the site of Columbus was the large earthen mound that gave this street its name. Prehistoric cultures now termed Adena and Hopewell built many ceremonial and burial mounds throughout the region.

Native Americans of the Erie nation lived in the area of present-day Columbus as early as 1300. Later Native American inhabitants included the Shawnee, Delaware, Iroquois, and Wyandots. European settlers arrived in the late 1700s. Columbus was founded in 1812, specifically to be the site of the state capital. It actually began serving as the capital in 1816 and was charted as a city in 1834. The city was named for Christopher Columbus.

Unlike neighboring cities such as Cleveland, Ohio, and Pittsburgh, Pennsylvania, Columbus was not a major destination during the United States' major periods of foreign immigration in the 19th and early 20th centuries. Nonetheless, German and Italian immigrants at one time formed sizeable communities in the city. In the 1860s, the population of the city was as much as one-third German. African Americans have lived in the city since its early years, and an influx of migrants from southern states greatly increased the city's black population in the early 20th century. Recent immigrants to the city include people from many diverse and far-flung locales, including Somalia, Laos, and Mexico.

Category people
Type participants

A vegetable stand at the North Market

Places to visit

German Village ❶

Settled by German immigrants, this historic district is the largest privately restored neighborhood in the United States. Renovated 19th- and early 20th-century buildings house shops, restaurants, and residences.

North Market ❷

Columbus's historic North Market, once primarily a farmer's market, now offers cuisine from around the world, as well as fresh fruits, vegetables, meats, and fish.

Franklin Park Conservatory and Franklin Park ❸

Franklin Park Conservatory is a leading horticultural education facility with displays including desert, tropical rain forest, Himalayan mountain, and Pacific Island environments. The park itself has a lake, a playground, basketball courts, and handsome trees and gardens.

The Topiary Garden ❹

This garden recreates a famous post-Impressionist painting by Georges Seurat in sculpted trees and shrubs. The display features topiary images of 54 people, eight boats,

Stained glass window in St. Mary's Catholic Church

Lake, Franklin Park

three dogs, a monkey, and a cat. The largest figure stands 12 feet tall.

The Topiary Garden

Georges Seurat, *A Sunday on La Grande Jatte – 1884*, 1884–86
Oil on canvas
81 ³/₄ x 121 ¹/₄ inches (207,6 x 308 cm)
Helen Birch Bartlett Memorial Collection, 1926.224
Collection of the Art Institute of Chicago

Columbus Zoo ❺

In 1956 the Columbus Zoo became the home of the first gorilla born in captivity. Today the zoo continues to be known for its innovations in breeding, conservation, and education.

Flamingo Island

Toledo & Ohio Central Railroad Station ❻

Built in 1895 and designed by the Columbus architectural firm Yost & Packard, this distinctive structure has a pagoda-style roof and octagonal towers. The building now houses a Volunteers of America thrift store and office. A two-story, barrel-vaulted interior space was once the waiting

Toledo & Ohio Central Railroad Station

room. In 1987, influential American architect Paul Rudolph surprised local architects and residents when he described this as his favorite building in Columbus.

Wexner Center for the Arts ❼

The Wexner Center for the Arts is the contemporary arts center at The Ohio State University. The landmark building was designed by Peter Eisenman and Richard Trott. The Wexner Center presents art exhibitions, dance, music, and theater performances, film/video screenings, and educational events for all ages. To find out about current and upcoming events, call (614) 292-3535 or visit the web site at www.wexarts.org.

Wexner Center

Downtown Columbus

amc 30 THEATRES
EASTON STATION

A closer look at some inner-city neighborhoods

Columbus consists of many neighborhoods, some close to downtown and considered part of the inner city and others spreading out into the suburbs. The three *Face Your World* program sites are in the inner-city neighborhoods known as the Near West Side (or Franklinton) and the Near East Side.

Near West Side / Franklinton

Franklinton, on the west bank of the Scioto River, was the first part of present-day Columbus to be settled by Europeans. Lucas Sullivant, a surveyor from Kentucky, laid out the town in 1797, well before Columbus was founded on the other side of the river. The village of 220 lots grew to be a community that is now three square miles in size and home to over 12,000 residents. According to the 2000 census, the population of this Near West Side community is approximately 74% white and 18% black, with smaller numbers of multiracial, Asian, Hispanic, and Native American residents.

Franklinton Post Office in the 1950s

The first post office in Franklinton, at 78 S. Gift Street, is commonly known as the Deardorf House. Weekly mail service began in 1805. Adam Hosack was the first postmaster and Andrew McElvain, at age 13, was the first mail carrier.

Franklinton Cemetery   8

Probably the oldest cemetery in Franklin County,

Monument in Franklinton Cemetery erected in 1931 to honor Lucas Sullivant and the early settlers

Franklinton Cemetery is located on land originally donated by Lucas Sullivant that is now part of an industrial area. The cemetery dates from 1799.

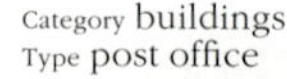

Category buildings
Type post office

Franklinton Post Office in 2002

Plaque on the monument

A plaque on the side of this monument commemorates the first Presbyterian Church, which was beside the cemetery. According to an old story, this church was used to store grain during the War of 1812. Water leaking through the roof made the grain expand – like oatmeal – and this caused the building to explode.

Presbyterian Church

Boys & Girls Clubs of Columbus Westside Unit   9

The building that now houses the Westside Unit of the Boys & Girls Clubs of Columbus was constructed in 1893 as the West Side Market House. It was a city market

Garden made as part of *Face Your World*

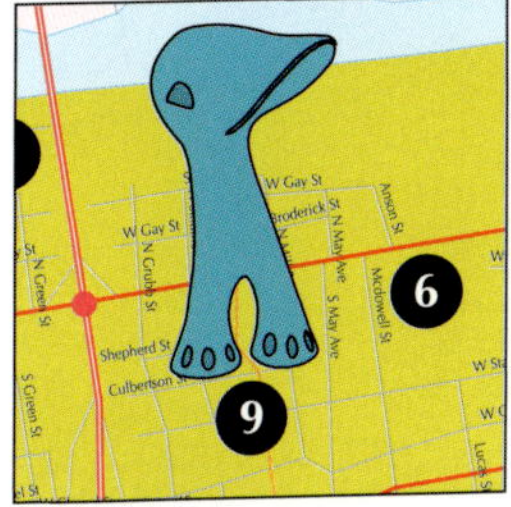

Meet Blake / Reanne / James / Ms. Molly

Blake Eshieel Rhea When taking a break from reading and playing games, 11-year-old Blake Rhea hangs out at the Boys & Girls Club. "It's like school but you're having fun!" Blake and her older sister Amber are enjoying their first year as club members.

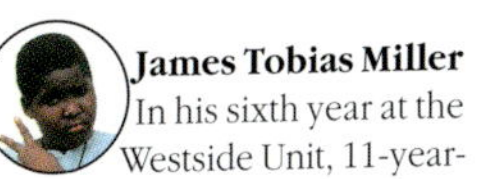

Reanne Seel Reanne Seel of Westerville, Ohio (a Columbus suburb), will either be a soccer star or a 4th grade math teacher when she grows up. She likes the *Face Your World* program because "you can make funny people and put everything where you want to." Starting this year, Reanne will play on a recreational soccer team.

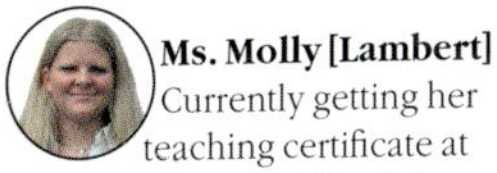

James Tobias Miller In his sixth year at the Westside Unit, 11-year-old James Miller continues to find the programming interesting and valuable. He particularly likes the *Smart Moves* program that teaches young people about the dangers of drug use. James also likes to draw, "mostly cats or dogs or animals in the cat or dog family. I also like to draw the Tasmanian Devil."

Ms. Molly [Lambert] Currently getting her teaching certificate at Urbana University, Ms. Molly enjoys working with the Children of the Future program. "I like that we use art to teach the program. The group of people I work with is great, and it gives me the opportunity to meet different people in the art community." When she's not at the Westside Unit, Ms. Molly is painting, drawing, swimming, and spending as much time as possible outdoors.

[see North Market: p.99], a gathering place for Franklinton residents, and the home of the West Market Athletic Club. The Boys Club of Columbus was formed in 1948 and first leased the building in 1949, for $1 per year. The club was open to boys exclusively until the late 1970s, when coed events began. In January 1990 the club's name was officially changed to the "Boys & Girls Clubs of Columbus, Inc." Boys & Girls Clubs of America are open every day, after school and on weekends, and offer kids a positive and affordable alternative to the streets. Dedicated to youth and staffed with full-time professionals, the clubs encourage young people to realize their full potential as creative, caring, and capable citizens of their community. Facilities at the Westside Unit include a library, a gymnasium, and a game room with ping pong, air hockey, and other games.

Game room

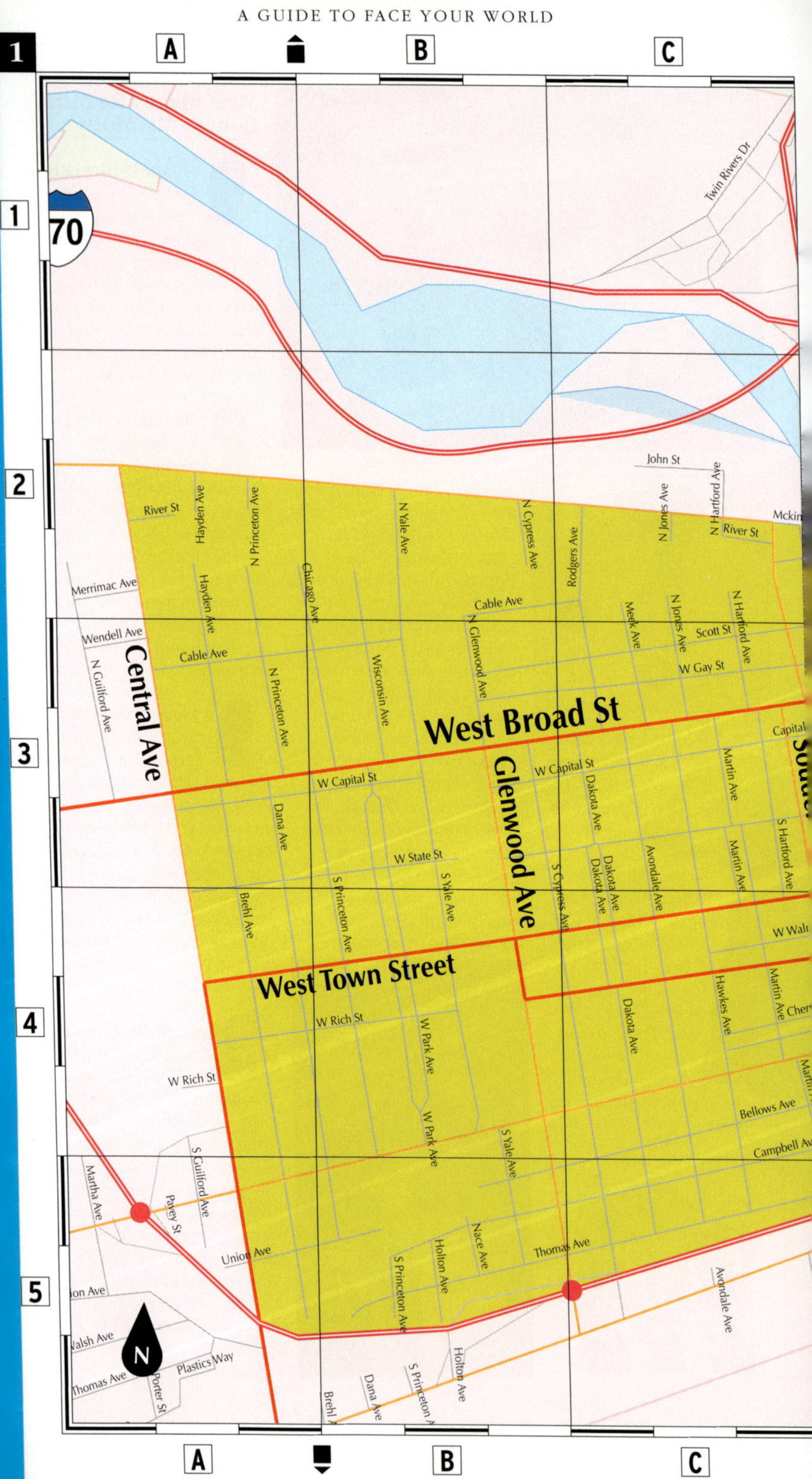
1
A
B
C
1
70
2
3
4
5
A
B
C
Twin Rivers Dr
John St
River St
Hayden Ave
N Princeton Ave
N Yale Ave
N Cypress Ave
Rodgers Ave
N Jones Ave
N Hartford Ave
Mckin
River St
Merrimac Ave
Hayden Ave
Chicago Ave
Cable Ave
Meek Ave
N Jones Ave
N Hartford Ave
Wendell Ave
N Glenwood Ave
Scott St
N Guilford Ave
Cable Ave
Central Ave
N Princeton Ave
Wisconsin Ave
W Gay St
West Broad St
Capital
Soude
W Capital St
Glenwood Ave
W Capital St
Martin Ave
Dana Ave
Dakota Ave
S Hartford Ave
W State St
S Yale Ave
S Cypress Ave
Dakota Ave
Avondale Ave
Martin Ave
Dakota Ave
Brehl Ave
S Princeton Ave
W Walr
West Town Street
W Rich St
Dakota Ave
Hawkes Ave
Martin Ave
Cher
W Park Ave
Martin Ave
W Rich St
Bellows Ave
S Yale Ave
Campbell Av
Martha Ave
S Guilford Ave
W Park Ave
Patey St
Nace Ave
Thomas Ave
Avondale Ave
Union Ave
Holton Ave
S Princeton Ave
on Ave
Walsh Ave
N
Thomas Ave
Plastics Way
Porter St
Brehl
Dana Ave
S Princeton Ave
Holton Ave

D
E
F
2
1
2
3
4
5
Neil Ave
Broadbelt Ln
Dublin Ave
Hocking St
Fletcher St
Hanover St
Cozzins St
Spring St
W Nagh
N Ludlow St
Blvd
Marco
W H
Marconi Blvd
W Lu
Toledo & Ohio Central Railroad Station 6
Franklinton Cemetery 8
Boys & Girls Clubs of Columbus Westside Unit 9
Dodge Skatepark 20
Franklinton Library 21
ley Ave
N River St
N Davis Ave
8
W Gay St
Broderick St
Anson St
W Gay St
N Grubb St
N May Ave
W Gay St
N Green St
Foos St
W Capital St
Rush Alley
Mcdowell St
S May Ave
6
Washington Blvd
N Davis Ave
Capital St
S Green St
Doyle St
Shepherd St
Culbertson St
W State St
St
9
W State St
W Chapel St
W Chapel St
Lucas St
W Chapel St
S Grubb St
S Davis Ave
Plato Dr
Minard Alley
Mead Alley
W Walnut St
W Walnut St
21
ouder Ave
S Green St
S Sandusky St
S Skidmore St
Cherry Dr
S May Ave
Cherry Dr
Levee St
S Civic Cente
S May Ave Ave
Plain Alley
y Alley
Plateau St
20
Sullivant Ave
Scioto Blvd
Short St
W
Maier Pl
Coolidge Dr
S Souder Ave
Polk Dr
Buchanan Dr
Van Buren Dr
Mount Calvary Ave
Pierce Dr
S Souder
Furnace St
W Whittier St
Harm
project site
photo stop
friday speaker
place on map
1
D
E
F

Near East Side

Columbus's Near East Side encompasses several distinct neighborhoods developed from the mid 19th century through the mid 20th century. Among them are the area now most frequently known as Olde Town East and the neighborhood along Mount Vernon Avenue, once the center of the local African American business community. According to the 2000 census, the area under the jurisdiction of Columbus's Near East Area Commission has a population of nearly 23,000. Over 81% percent of area residents are black and 13.5% are white, with smaller numbers of multiracial, Hispanic, Asian, and Native American residents.

Mount Vernon Ave. in 2002

Poindexter Village 🔟

Built under the direction of the Columbus Metropolitan Housing Authority between 1939 and 1941, Poindexter Village became the third low-income public housing project in the United States – and the first public housing project in Columbus. It was named after Columbus's first African American city councilman, the Reverend James P. Poindexter (1819–1907) of the Second Baptist Church. President Franklin Roosevelt attended the opening ceremonies. The project was built on the site of a neighborhood known as the Blackberry Patch, which was home to African Americans who migrated from the South at the turn of the 20th century. The new construction displaced many residents of the Blackberry Patch, who were scattered all over the city.

Mount Vernon Avenue 11️⃣

In the 1940s and 1950s Mount Vernon Avenue was a lively place with varied stores, restaurants, and clubs. When new highways isolated the community, many businesses closed and buildings were abandoned and boarded up.

Artist Aminah Robinson (back row, second from right) told the kids about the history of Mount Vernon Avenue and Poindexter Village as depicted in images from her book *A Street Called Home*.

The King Arts Complex 12️⃣

The King Arts Complex offers performing arts, cultural, and educational programs that celebrate the significant contributions and artistic heritage of African Americans throughout the world. The oldest part of the building dates from 1925 and was originally a lodge and theater for artists and residents of the Near East Side

The King Arts Complex

Marion M. Richardson, *The parade*, 1950, Courtesy of Florence Richardson   Mount Vernon Avenue in 1950.

of Columbus. The KAC provides space for the training of the artist members of the Children of the Future program. To find out about events at the KAC, visit the web site at www.thekingartscomplex.com or call (614) 645-5464.

Sawyer Recreation Center ⓭

Sawyer Recreation Center is one of 28 neighborhood recreation centers administered by Columbus's Recreation and Parks Department. Located near The King Arts Complex and Mount Vernon Avenue, Sawyer opened in the 1970s

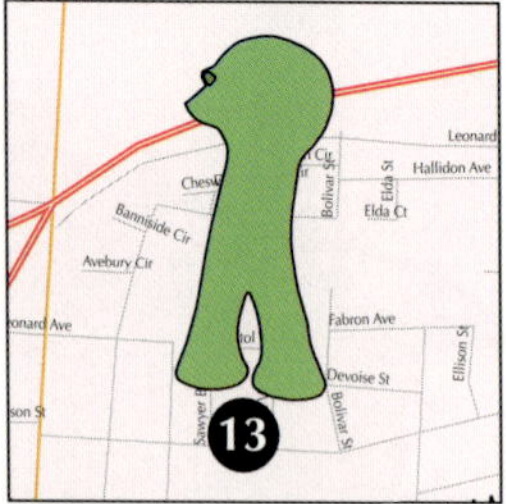

and was renovated in 1997 to become a multigenerational recreation center.

Its senior citizens center offers crafts, physical fitness programs, and music and dancing. Activities for children, youths, and adults include basketball, tennis (on newly constructed courts), fine arts, dancing, and theater.

In addition to the Children of the Future program, Sawyer hosts Cap City Kids, an after-school homework assistance program funded by the City of Columbus Department of Education. A food pantry is also located at the site.

Sawyer Recreation Center entrance

Meet Shalam / Taija / Mr. Jeff

Shalam Majors
Shalam Majors, a fourth grader at Arlington Park Elementary School, is looking forward to being a college professor when she grows up. For now she is enjoying her summer afternoons at Sawyer Recreation Center. In her free time Shalam likes to color, draw, and play Play Station 2.

Taija Moore
Six-year-old Taija Moore's favorite things about summer are peanut butter and jelly sandwiches, chocolate ice cream, and going to the beach. This fall she will be in the first grade at Oakland Park Elementary School and is looking forward to playing freeze tag on the playground with her friends Carmen, Jasmine, and Tanisha.

Mr. Jeff [Ostrowski]
In his second year with the Children of the Future program, Mr. Jeff thinks it's "the best job ever in the world." In his free time Mr. Jeff likes to read about religion and philosophy. You might also catch him listening to some of his favorite music by artists such as Elton John, Billy Joel, and local rock group Shaving Nancy.

Street furniture made as part of *Face Your World*

Olde Town East or African Village? ⑭

This neighborhood of houses built in the late 19th and early 20th centuries is undergoing major changes. Some of the large houses on Bryden Road and adjacent streets have been extensively renovated, while others are dilapidated or boarded up. As property values and housing costs go up, some long-time residents can no longer afford to live here. One name for the neighborhood, Olde Town East, emphasizes the age of its historic buildings. But Baba Olugbala, an artist who lives in the area, suggests that the neighborhood should be called African Village instead, a name that would honor the African Americans who have lived here, just like the name German Village reflects the cultural heritage of that neighborhood.

Sign at Baba Olugbala's house

Blackburn Recreation Center ⑮

Blackburn Recreation Center is another of the 28 neighborhood recreation centers administered by Columbus's Recreation and Parks Department. Located just off Bryden Road, Blackburn offers arts, sports and physical fitness, and educational activities for children and adults. Dedicated in 1969, the complex features one of the city's outdoor public swimming pools, a large

Diorama made as part of *Face Your World*

gymnasium with an indoor running track, a boxing room, and photography and ceramics studios. The Inner-City Games program at the site was opened in 2000 by famed bodybuilder Arnold Schwarzenegger.

Swimming pool

Meet Quincy / Brittany / Deanna / Ms. Linda

Quincy Keith
"I like the bus because it gets me off the couch to play," says 13-year-old Quincy Keith. Aside from boxing and making videos on the computer at school, Quincy likes to spend his time in the art room. He enjoys any kind of art project that encourages his creative abilities.

Brittany Coffey
Brittany Coffey, who is 10, is in her third year in the Children of the Future program. In her free time she loves to play basketball, tag, and make up cheers with her friends. "When I grow up I want to be a basketball player, a doctor, and a singer."

Deanna Ratleff
When in school, fourth grader Deanna Ratleff feels most at home in the art room, the library, and the computer lab. She likes to write stories, play games on the computer, read her favorite Dr. Seuss books, swim, and just have fun.

Ms. Linda [Miller]
After receiving her bachelor's degree in speech and hearing science from the University of Florida and several adventures abroad, Ms. Linda has returned to Ohio to work with the Children of the Future program. She says the best thing about the program is working with the kids. A break from the art room gives Ms. Linda the chance to enjoy cycling, eating spicy salsa, and working with mixed media and found objects on her own art projects.

1
A
B
C

The Topiary Garden 4
Poindexter Village 10
Mount Vernon Avenue 11
The King Arts Complex 12
Sawyer Recreation Center 13
Olde Town East or African Village 14
Blackburn Recreation Center 15
Jim Arter's garden 18

Curtis Ave
Jefferson Pl
Leonard Ave
Atcheson St
Hamilton Ave
Buckingham St
Grove St
Hamilton Ave
Edward St
N Garfield Ave

1

Jack Gibbs Blvd
Jack Gibbs Blvd

2

N 6th St
N Grant Ave
Mccoy St
Kellogg St
Grove St
Edward St
Mount Vernon Ave
N 11th St
Sisco Alley
Jefferson Ave
Sisco Alley
Cosmo Alley
St Clair Ave
N Garfield Ave
E Spring St
Garfield Pl
Kiefer St
Garfield Pl

N 5th St
Burr St
N 6th St
Neilston St
Milton Alley
Kelly Alley
Connell Ave
N 9th St
N Washington Ave
E Naghten St
N Everett Alley
Kiefer St
N 11th St

3

N Lazelle St
Mckee St
N Young St
E Lafayette St
N 5th St
N Kelly Alley
Connell Alley
Kelly Alley
Freeman Ave
N Everett Alley
Boone St
N 11th St
Zimmerman Ct
Boone St
Hamilton Ave

N 5th St
Normandy Ave
N 6th St
E Gay St
E Gay St
Connell Pl
Hutton Pl
Avon Pl
Avon Pl

E Elm St
Sells Pl
S 9th St
S Everett Alley
Agate
S Garfield Ave

4

E Lynn St
E Capital St
Oak St
Wales Alley
Elliott Alley
Franklin Ave
Lester Dr

N
S Young St
S 5th St
E State St
S 6th St
Library Park Ct
Selina Alley
Calloway Alley
S 11th St

4

E Chapel St
Street
E Walnut St
Waldo Alley
E Rich St
Bryden Alley

5

project site
photo stop
friday speaker
1 place on map

E Cherry St
E Noble St
Cowling Alley
Waldo Alley
Marshall Alley
E Mound St
Hamm
Mcallis

A
B
C

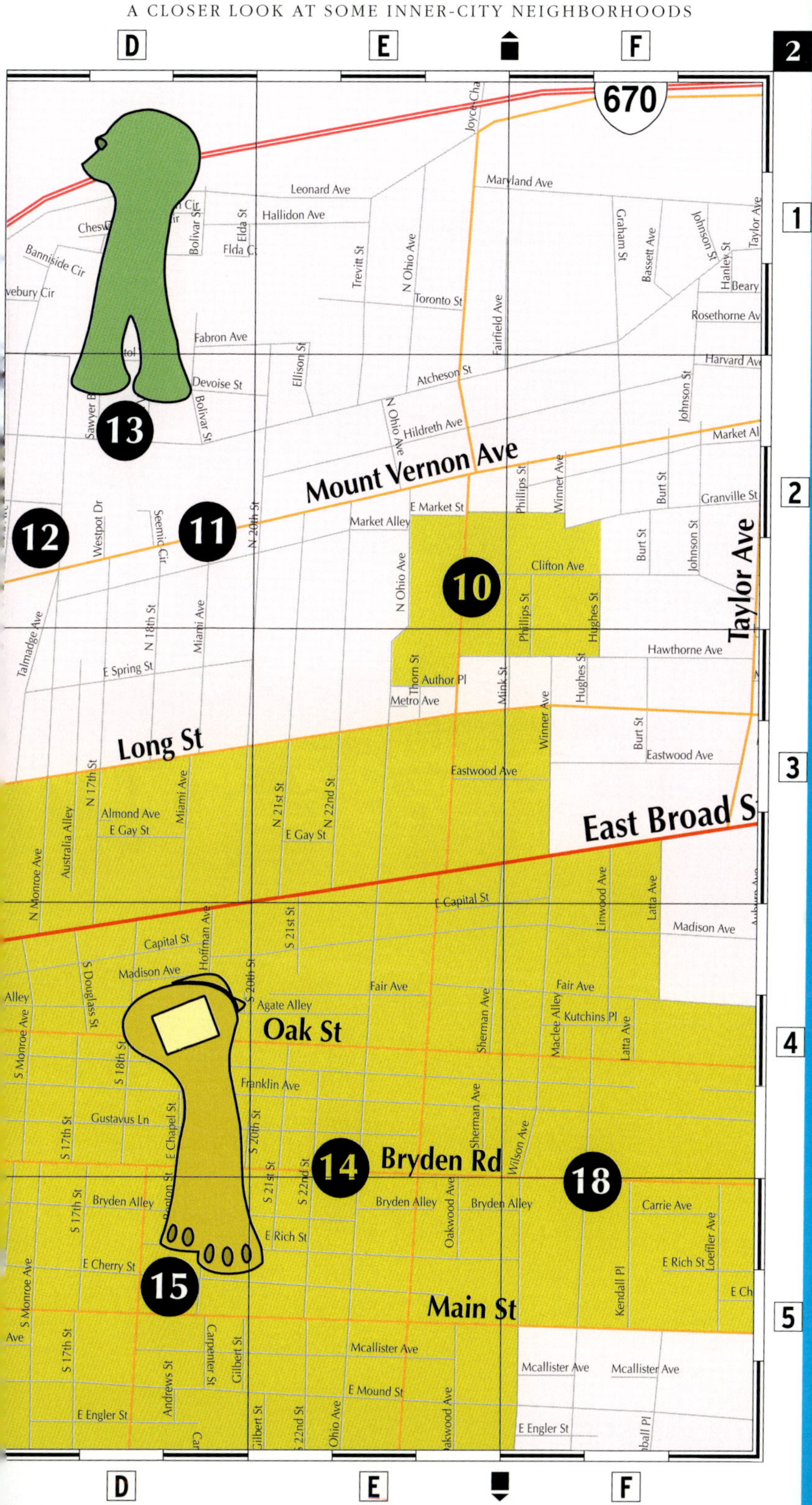
D
E
F
2
1
2
3
4
5
670
Maryland Ave
Leonard Ave
Hallidon Ave
Graham St
Bassett Ave
Johnson St
Hanley St
Taylor Ave
Beary
Rosethorne Av
Chesw
Cir
Bolivar St
Elda St
Elda Ct
Trevitt St
N Ohio Ave
Toronto St
Fairfield Ave
Bannside Cir
vebury Cir
Fabron Ave
Ellison St
Atcheson St
Harvard Ave
Devoise St
Bolivar St
N Ohio Ave
Hildreth Ave
Johnson St
Market Al
Sawyer B
13
Mount Vernon Ave
Winner Ave
Phillips St
Burt St
Granville St
Westpot Dr
Seemic Cir
N 20th St
E Market St
Market Alley
Clifton Ave
Burt St
Johnson St
12
11
10
Taylor Ave
N Ohio Ave
Phillips St
Hughes St
Talmadge Ave
N 19th St
N 18th St
Miami Ave
Hawthorne Ave
E Spring St
Thorn St
Author Pl
Hughes St
Metro Ave
Mink St
Winner Ave
Burt St
Eastwood Ave
Long St
N 17th St
Miami Ave
Eastwood Ave
East Broad S
Almond Ave
E Gay St
N 21st St
N 22nd St
E Gay St
Australia Alley
N Monroe Ave
Linwood Ave
Latta Ave
E Capital St
Madison Ave
Capital St
Hoffman Ave
S 21st St
N 20th St
Madison Ave
S Douglass St
Fair Ave
Sherman Ave
Fair Ave
Alley
N Monroe Ave
Agate Alley
Maclee Alley
Kutchins Pl
Latta Ave
Oak St
S 18th St
Franklin Ave
S Monroe Ave
Gustavus Ln
E Chapel St
Sherman Ave
Wilson Ave
S 17th St
enton St
S 20th St
14
Bryden Rd
18
S 21st St
N 22nd St
Bryden Alley
Bryden Alley
Bryden Alley
Carrie Ave
S 17th St
Bryden Alley
E Rich St
Oakwood Ave
Kendall Pl
Loeffler Ave
E Cherry St
E Rich St
E Ch
15
S Monroe Ave
Main St
E
S 17th St
Carpenter St
Gilbert St
Mcallister Ave
Mcallister Ave
Mcallister Ave
Andrews St
E Mound St
E Engler St
Gilbert St
N 22nd St
Ohio Ave
Oakwood Ave
E Engler St
Car
D
E
F

Getting around Columbus

Columbus is best visited by car. Some areas of the city and suburbs lack public transportation, but highways lead to nearly every neighborhood.

Two major Interstates converge on Columbus.

I-71 links Columbus with Cleveland to the northeast and Cincinnati to the southwest. I-70 takes drivers west to Indiana and east to West Virginia and Pennsylvania. The I-270 outer belt surrounds the city and links outlying suburbs. The busiest times to drive are during the rush hours, between 7 and 9 am and 4 and 6 pm.

👉 Updated **16** traffic reports are given by the City of Columbus Traffic Management Center on TV and radio stations. Visit http://pavingtheway.org for updates on road construction and to view traffic cams on the web.

Public transportation

👉 Columbus's public transportation system consists of a bus network operated by the Central Ohio Transit Authority (COTA). Service tends to be most active in the central city and during rush hours. Late night and weekend service is more limited. Large, 40-foot-long

Car made as part of *Face Your World*

buses service main routes; smaller, connector buses (ABI buses) travel on less busy routes and ones that include narrow streets. For information about COTA fares, routes, and schedules, phone (614) 228-1776 or look at www.cota.com.

17 Driving a car in Columbus

As in most American cities, the infrastructure in Columbus is made for having a car. Traffic moves at an average of 25 mph on city streets, and parking is easy to find. Most residents of Columbus get around by car. Even in the city, many people drive powerful Sport Utility Vehicles or SUVs.

Columbus on foot

If you want you can walk in Columbus, although the city does not really have an active pedestrian culture. The Short North (an area of restaurants, galleries, and shops clustered along High Street just north of downtown) is one of the relatively few neighborhoods where people embrace sidewalk strolling as a pastime.

Category people
Type pedestrian

Getting around Face Your World

From June 17 through August 16, 2002 a specially designed and equipped COTA bus traveled the streets of Columbus. Decorated with an interpretation of Columbus cityscapes and emblazoned *Face Your World*, the bus was outfitted with computers as a digital lab. The bus was part of the project *Face Your World*, in which children donned the mantle of city planners as they took part in a work of art that brought together public transportation, computer technology, and creative thinking. For information on *Face Your World*, call (614) 292-3535 or visit www.wexarts.org.

The *Face Your World* bus

The interior of the bus was modified to fit the needs of the project. The furniture to house the computer stations was custom-made by Matt Clausen.

Interior of the bus

The Face Your World bus

Mondays, Tuesdays, and Wednesdays between 2 pm and 4:30 pm, the *Face Your World* bus was on the road, taking children between the three program sites: the Boys & Girls Clubs of Columbus Westside Unit, Blackburn Recreation Center, and Sawyer Recreation Center. On Mondays, children from the Westside Unit traveled to either Blackburn or Sawyer to meet other children and participate in programs. On Tuesdays, kids from Blackburn traveled to one of the other sites, and on Wednesdays, it was children from Sawyer's turn to travel on the *Face Your World* bus.

The bus stops

The *Face Your World* bus stopped at large, colorful public sculptures installed on the grounds of the three program sites. Made by Dutch artist Joep van Lieshout, these playful creatures seemed part human and part animal. Inside each bus stop was a video monitor that displayed the bus route and images of the neighborhoods created by participating children.

Bus stop at Sawyer

In 1995, Joep van Lieshout created Atelier van Lieshout, a workshop where about 25 artists work cooperatively to produce art works that are practical, simple, and sturdy. Their products vary from polyester furniture to brightly colored mobile living units.

Fabricating the bus stops at Atelier van Lieshout

Passport

Riding the Face Your World bus

To ride the *Face Your World* bus you had to be ages 5 to 12 and attending one of the drop-in programs operated by the Children of the Future program at the Boys & Girls Clubs Westside Unit, Blackburn Recreation Center, or Sawyer Recreation Center. You also needed a signed permission slip and passport.

Passports

A special document allowed unlimited travel on the *Face Your World* bus between the three program sides. Passports could be obtained at the Boys & Girls Clubs Westside Unit, Blackburn Recreation Center, and Sawyer Recreation Center. For a passport children needed a passport-sized photo (taken at the program site) and a parent or guardian's signature on the permission slip in the back. The children collected stamps and stickers in their passports every time they rode the bus. The passport number was each child's personal access code for using the Interactor.

What Is "Children of the Future"?

Children of the Future is an arts and public safety AmeriCorps program designed and managed by the Greater Columbus Arts Council for youth ages 5 to 12. Programs are free and take place at inner-city recreation and community centers, after school and during the summer. Two to four artists work in teams to plan and conduct activities in dance, creative writing, music, theater, and visual arts. The program uses art to create a safe haven and emphasizes the development of constructive communication and conflict resolution skills as tools for coping with social pressure and temptations. Children of the Future is a Columbus-based project of AmeriCorps, an initiative of the Corporation for National and Community Service. The Greater Columbus Arts Council's Community Arts Education Program coordinates Children of the Future in cooperation with the City of Columbus Recreation and Parks Department, the Department of Public Safety, and other program partners, including the Boys & Girls Clubs of Columbus, Inc.

Bus routes: Photo stops

Each day the *Face Your World* bus traveled a different route between the three program sites. The bus stopped on the way at various places in the city, allowing the children to experience these sites and take digital images to use in the Interactor or add to its library. Bus route maps with the stops marked were available at the front of the bus.

Route 21, 22, 23:

Volunteers of America, 379 W. Broad St. [see: p.100]

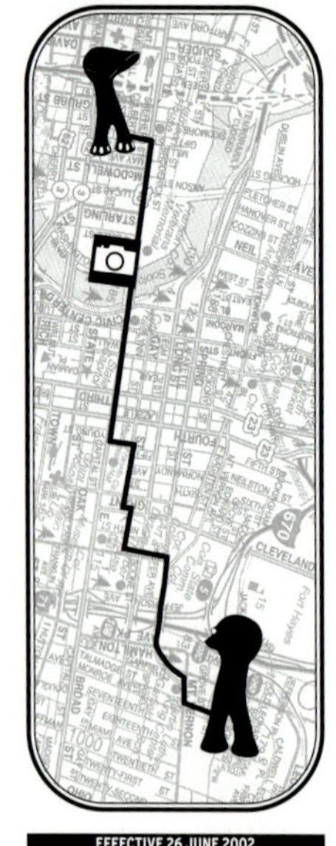

Route 31, 32, 33:

North Market, 59 Spruce St. [see: p.99]

Route 41, 42, 43:

Franklinton Cemetery, Souder Ave. [see: p.102]

Route 51, 52, 53:

Jim Arter's garden, 1424 Bryden Rd.

Jim Arter transformed the bare and empty lot next to his house into a beautiful town garden.

Route 61, 62, 63:

City of Columbus Police Impound Lot, 400 W. Whittier St.

Impound lot

Every city needs a secure storage area for vehicles that have been impounded, seized, or are being held for investigative purposes. At the impound lot you'll find every make and model under the sun.

Kids listening to Sergeant Harrisson

Route 71, 72, 73:

Dodge Skatepark, 667 Sullivant Ave.

Built in 1991, Dodge Skatepark is a favorite spot for skateboarders, roller bladers, and bicyclists. The park was sponsored by the Recreation and Parks Department and designed by Bill Minadeo, Donney Humes, and the late Frank Hawk, pro-skater Tony Hawk's dad.

Skateboarder Craig Dransfield jumping

Route 81, 82, 83:

Franklin Park and Franklin Park Conservatory, 1777 East Broad St. [see: p.99]

The Interactor

The Interactor is a specifically designed computer program for children who live in the neighborhoods around the three Children of the Future sites participating in *Face Your World*. The virtual world of the Interactor was constructed from a library of over 500 digital photographs of these neighborhoods. Participating children used a digital camera to photograph various people and places they visited on the bus and during the programs. The children could download their photographs into the computer program and manipulate, combine, and recombine their photographs to create visions of their city.

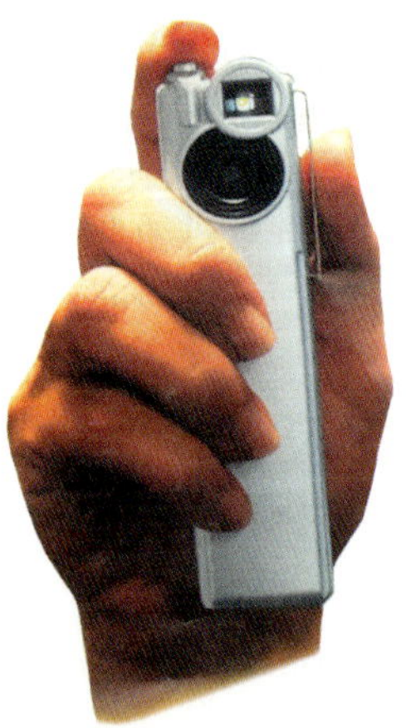
digital camera

The PenCam Trio is a digital camera, PC camera, and digital camcorder in one. It weighs around 70 grams and is barely bigger than a pen. You can make 26 high-resolution images of 640 x 480 pixels or 107 low-resolution images of 320 x 240 pixels.

A network

The Interactor was set up on a network of computers on the bus, so that each player encountered other players in the game. To enter the virtual world of the Interactor the children must "interact" with others, so the virtual world was also a shared world. The game-like software encouraged children to explore their ideas about their neighborhoods and to consider their relationship to their community and its interconnections to the larger society. Questions posed in the program asked children to make decisions about their environment collaboratively and to draw on their experiences and values in the decision-making process. The children communicated online in a chat space, where they could discuss decisions or just send each other messages.

The design of the Interactor was the result of collaboration between *Face Your World* creator Jeanne van Heeswijk, philosopher and poet Maaike Engelen [see: p.79], and V2_Lab, a part of V2_Organisation. V2_Organisation was founded in 1981 by a group of multimedia artists in the Netherlands who were interested in exploring the relationship between art and computer technology. They provide opportunities for artists, scientists, and computer programmers to develop creative uses of computer technology and other electronic media.

V2_Lab, Rotterdam, The Netherlands

Using the Interactor

Kids entered the Interactor by typing in their name and passport number. A tutorial program showed the various tools and functions of the game.

Tutorial

You know your neighborhood pretty well, because you live there. Maybe sometimes you like it a whole lot. Maybe sometimes you hate it. Maybe sometimes you don't think about it at all. However you feel, with this Interactor you can change your world.

Max Moore, who served as our *Face Your World* avatar, is Project Coordinator for Columbus Mayor Michael B. Coleman's Downtown Business Plan. The plan aims to create new investment opportunities and bring life to Columbus's central city.

Hello, I'm Max Moore. I work with the mayor's office in Columbus as a downtown planner.

Building the world is what we do all the time.

Now we need to build more than ever to change this city.

We need to create more places to go to and hang out in.

We need to build houses and shops, parks, half pipes, benches, lampposts, and a lot of roads!

It is hard work.

We can make mistakes.

We work in a team all the time.

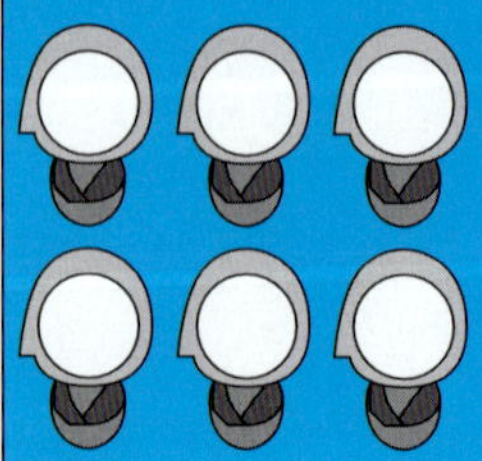

I really need new team players.

Maybe you have plans I never thought about. I need your help to find out how you want the world around you to be. Help me build your future world.

We have an hour and a half to plan.

Come on, let's face it!

Here is your world.

The arrows on your keyboard make you walk.

Jump in and change things to the way you would like to see them. If you do not like something, click on it. Put it on your drawing board. Now you can change it: cut, color, draw, rotate, or erase it. Need something different? Look in the library. Or use your own pictures. Load them.

Choose what you need.

You can also cut, color, draw, rotate, or write on it, to make it your own way.

Finally, tell what the picture means to you before you add it to the library.

Back in your world, place the picture on a box or object.

Put it to where you like it in your city.

Make it bigger or smaller, rotate it, move it.

Chatting

You are not alone in the world.

You will run into each other.

Not everything can happen the way you want it to.

Sometimes you'll really need to think just for yourself.

Sometimes you'll need ideas from the whole group.

You have to chat with each other about your plans.

Although you'll start to build in a place for yourself, you'll very quickly run out of space and will meet others to build with.

Remember, you are building together.

I will be around every 10 minutes.

I will ask questions to help you.

Or to let you know when you try something that won't work in this world. We have an hour and a half to face the world and change it your way.

Then you need to present it.

So I can find out if I can use some of your ideas in the future. You can also show your work on the bus stops. [see bus stops: p.114]

So others will know how you face your world and maybe want it that way too.

What is an avatar?

An avatar is a graphical representation of a character in a virtual world. In *Face Your World*, an icon representing Max Moore, our city planner, appeared in the program asking questions and helping resolve conflicts that might arise as participating children investigated shared virtual space.

While working on the network, the children were also represented by avatars. The children could upload the avatar with their own face. This way they could see each other navigate through the world.

Avatar running

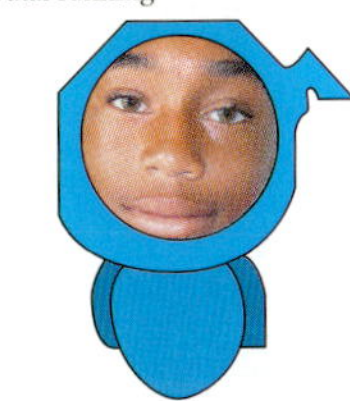
Avatar talking

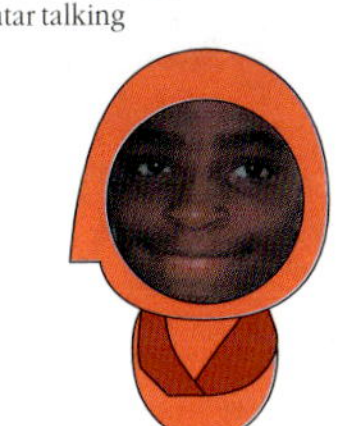
Avatar waiting

Avatar building

The library

The foundation of the library consisted of over 500 images taken in Columbus by Jeanne van Heeswijk and Rolf Engelen. During the course of the project, the participating children added another 500 images that they took themselves. The library was organized in seven categories: buildings, people, vehicles, street furniture, animals, nature, and grounds. See pages 156–171 for a selection of the images.

Category **buildings**
Type **family restaurant**

Category **nature**
Type **tree**

Category **vehicles**
Type **motorcycle**

Category **people**
Type **participant**

A community program: Speakers and field trips

In *Face Your World*, the emphasis was on children's understanding of the complexity of the urban environment in which they live. The children investigated the planning process and issues addressed by urban planners, as well as such topics as land use, public transportation, air pollution, and the effects of growth and change on a community. During the nine-week *Face Your World* program Fridays were usually the days for speakers and field trips, offering opportunities for the children to hear the ideas of people who work in and with the city on a daily basis.

June 17–19: Damon Taylor, photographer, "Introductory Photo Workshop"
June 21: Aminah Brenda Lynn Robinson, artist, "History of Poindexter Village" [see: p.106]
June 28: Brenda Dutton, historian, "History of Franklinton" [see: p.102]
July 05: David Efland, city planner, "Planning a City"

The children learned about city planning by playing the roles of mayor, developer, and citizens in a game. "The people ask the mayor for a bus," one said.

July 12: Norm Burns, German Village resident and local historian, "A Video/Walking Tour" [see: p.99]
July 19: Jim Kerr, water plant operator, "City of Columbus Division of Water"

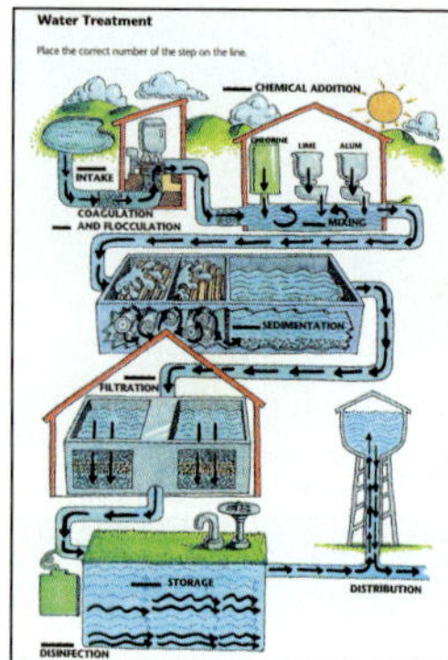

Water treatment

July 26: Columbus Zoo [see: p.100]
August 02: Gary Holt, traffic center manager, "The City of Columbus Traffic Management Center"

Controlling traffic at the Traffic Management Center

August 09: Jim Daley, COTA public affairs manager, "Public Transportation: Past, Present, and Future" [see: p.113]

Body shop

August 16: Closing Party at Blackburn Recreation Center.

How do kids see their world?

The worlds the children created were theirs to take home when they left the Interactor: they could make color printouts of the images they created. The children's work

also could be seen at the bus stops
[see: p. 114] and on the web site
www.faceyourworld.net.

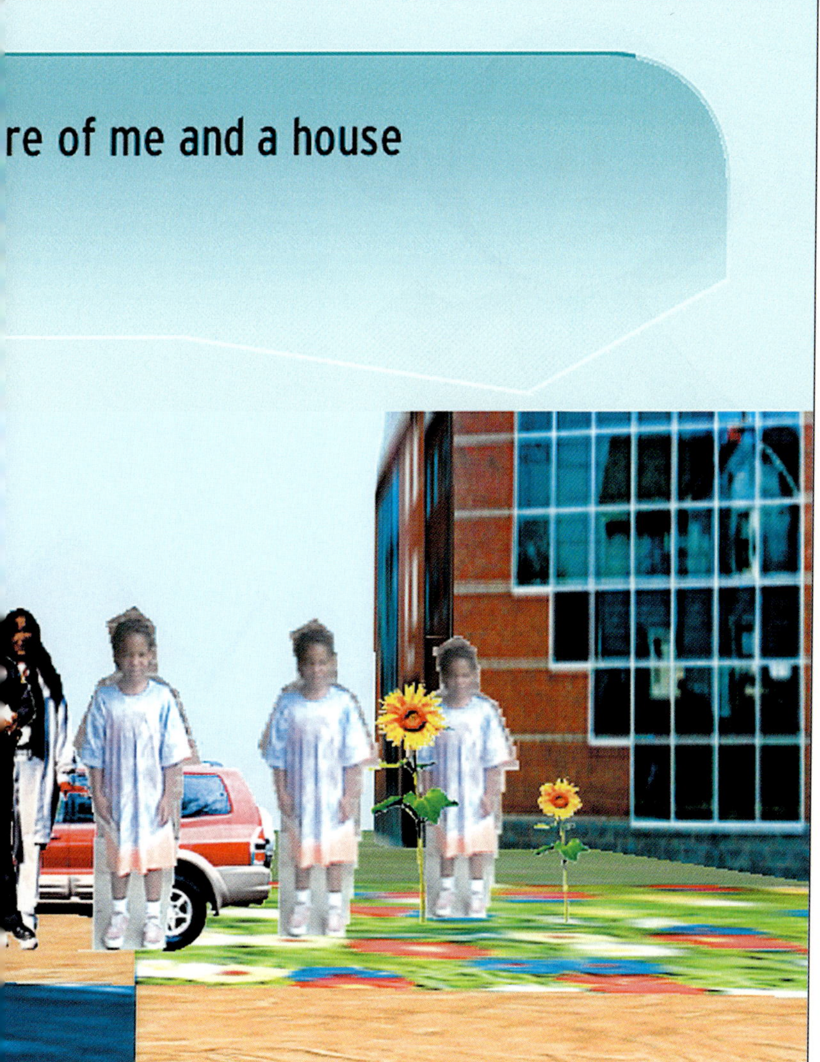

jelly ho

house w

big kitty and man

DJ BUR
Donatos Pizza
THICKER CRUST!
ZESTY SAUCE!

- DYNAMITE KID JULY 3, 2002

RAVEN

WORLD
eve
SUPER PREMIUM · HAND DIPPED

sports

Tremay

taylors

rld
Supplies
PETCO
& Fish

miss m
miss m
SCHOOL

elles first jump
conplans
WHO ME?
FACE YOUR WORLD

Donatos Pizza
NEW PIZZA!
THICKER CRUST!
ZESTY SAUCE!

141
Famous
Footwear

a house
Pizza
ZESTY
SAUCE!
forna
B.C
$1,000

a day
$1,000 $1,000
For For
sale sale

A FOOD
LAS MARAVILLAS
Mexican Market
White Castle
Domino's Pizza

RKET WHICH CAMERON WILL EAT!!!1
McDonald's
Fish & Chips
Bob Evans
RESTAURANT

A PLAY
MARINO'S SEAFOOD
Fish & Chips
cDonald's
Pizza

OUND
STOP

shanied

oves her family

MY WO

drey
STOP

JANAE'

'ORLD

Category buildings
Type house

Category buildings
Type store

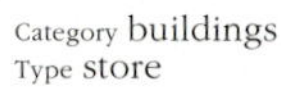
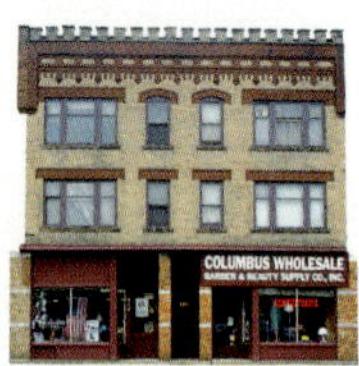

Category buildings
Type fast food restaurant

Category buildings
Type fast food restaurant

Category buildings
Type medical center

Category buildings
Type restaurant

Category buildings
Type multistory house

Category buildings
Type duplex

Category buildings
Type school

Category buildings
Type shotgun house

Category buildings
Type restaurant

Category buildings
Type mexican market

Category buildings
Type house

Category buildings
Type hotel

Category buildings
Type office building

Category **buildings**
Type shop

Category **buildings**
Type victorian house

Category **buildings**
Type office building

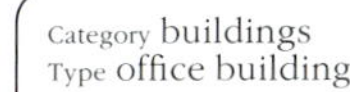

Category **buildings**
Type fast food restaurant

Category **buildings**
Type apartment building

Category **buildings**
Type greenhouse

Category **buildings**
Type church

Category **buildings**
Type coffee shop

Category **buildings**
Type store

Category **buildings**
Type book store

Category **buildings**
Type animal hospital

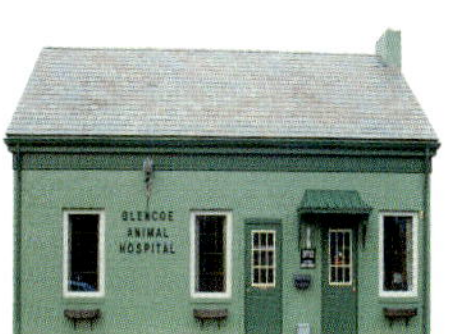

Category **buildings**
Type church

Category **buildings**
Type office building

Category **buildings**
Type house

Category **buildings**
Type house

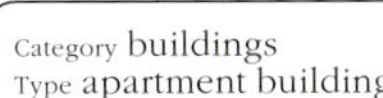

Category **buildings**
Type **pet supply store**

Category **buildings**
Type **apartment**

Category **buildings**
Type **house**

Category **buildings**
Type **house**

Category **buildings**
Type **church**

Category **buildings**
Type **fast food restaurant**

Category **buildings**
Type **cement factory**

Category **buildings**
Type **church**

Category **buildings**
Type **office building**

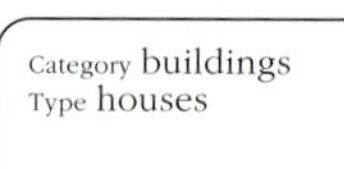

Category **buildings**
Type **recreation center**

Category **buildings**
Type **houses**

Category **buildings**
Type **family restaurant**

Category **buildings**
Type **house**

Category **buildings**
Type **house**

Category **buildings**
Type **highrise apartment**

Category buildings
Type apartment

Category buildings
Type fire station

Category buildings
Type condo

Category buildings
Type food stand

Category buildings
Type museum

Category buildings
Type apartment

Category buildings
Type office building

Category buildings
Type house

Category buildings
Type house

Category buildings
Type house

Category buildings
Type landmark

Category buildings
Type thrift store

Category buildings
Type church

Category buildings
Type office building

Category buildings
Type theater

Category **vehicles**
Type **police car**

Category **vehicles**
Type **postal truck**

Category **vehicles**
Type **suv**

Category **vehicles**
Type **fire truck**

Category **vehicles**
Type **ambulance**

Category **vehicles**
Type **bloodmobile**

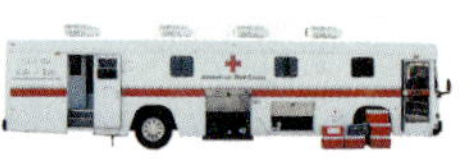

Category **vehicles**
Type **stretch limo**

Category **vehicles**
Type **touring car**

Category **vehicles**
Type **vintage car**

Category **vehicles**
Type **police car**

Category **vehicles**
Type **motorcycle**

Category **vehicles**
Type **yellow cab**

Category **vehicles**
Type **school bus**

Category **vehicles**
Type **truck**

Category **vehicles**
Type **car**

Category **vehicles**
Type **truck**

Category **vehicles**
Type **SUV**

Category **vehicles**
Type **vintage car**

Category **vehicles**
Type **school bus**

Category **vehicles**
Type **car**

Category **vehicles**
Type **car**

Category **vehicles**
Type **suv**

Category **vehicles**
Type **pick up**

Category **vehicles**
Type **car**

Category **vehicles**
Type **car**

Category **vehicles**
Type **FedEx truck**

Category **vehicles**
Type **bicycle**

Category **vehicles**
Type **bmx**

Category **vehicles**
Type **golf cart**

Category **vehicles**
Type **car**

Category people
Type jogger

Category people
Type rollerblader

Category people
Type pedestrian

Category people
Type pedestrian

Category people
Type wheelchair user

Category people
Type supporter

Category people
Type co-curator

Category people
Type photographer

Category people
Type dog walker

Category people
Type squatter

Category people
Type police officer

Category people
Type nurse

Category people
Type pedestrian

Category people
Type artist

Category people
Type teacher

Category **people**
Type teacher

Category **people**
Type teacher

Category **people**
Type teacher

Category **people**
Type teacher

Category **people**
Type teacher

Category **people**
Type police officer

Category **people**
Type programmer

Category **people**
Type participant

Category **people**
Type basketball player

Category **people**
Type bmxer

Category **people**
Type basketball players

Category **people**
Type football player

Category **people**
Type skater

Category **people**
Type participant

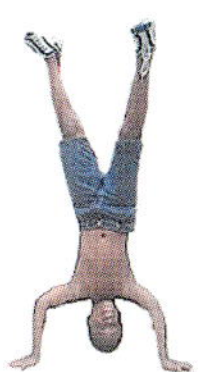

Category **people**
Type teacher

Category **people**
Type participant

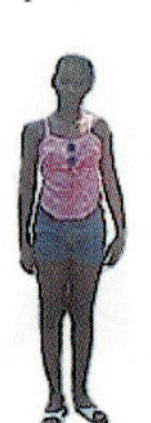

Category **people**
Type spectators

Category **people**
Type bus driver

Category **people**
Type participants and shopkeeper

Category **people**
Type educator

Category **people**
Type participant

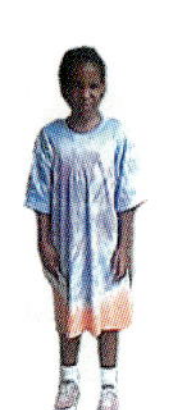

Category **people**
Type participant

Category **people**
Type participant

Category **people**
Type participant

Category **people**
Type participant

Category **people**
Type participant

Category **people**
Type participant

Category **people**
Type educator

Category **people**
Type participant

Category **people**
Type participant

Category people
Type participant

Category people
Type participant

Category people
Type participant

Category people
Type participants

Category people
Type participant

Category people
Type participant

Category people
Type participant

Category people
Type doughboy

Category people
Type participant

Category people
Type participant

Category people
Type participant

Category people
Type participants

Category people
Type participants

Category people
Type participant

Category people
Type participant

Category **nature**
Type bush

Category **nature**
Type boulder

Category **nature**
Type shrub

Category **nature**
Type tree

Category **nature**
Type tree

Category **nature**
Type neon tree

Category **nature**
Type flower

Category **nature**
Type flower

Category **nature**
Type plant

Category **nature**
Type plant

Category **nature**
Type fruit

Category **nature**
Type waterplants

Category **nature**
Type tree

Category **nature**
Type planter

Category **nature**
Type topiary figures

Category **animals**
Type dog

Category **animals**
Type dog

Category **animals**
Type dog

Category **animals**
Type rabbit

Category **animals**
Type bird

Category **animals**
Type fox

Category **animals**
Type bird

Category **animals**
Type dog

Category **animals**
Type seagull

Category **animals**
Type crash bandicoot

Category **animals**
Type cat

Category **animals**
Type lion

Category **animals**
Type dog

Category **animals**
Type fish

Category **animals**
Type teddy bears

Category street furniture
Type phone booth

Category street furniture
Type public art

Category street furniture
Type exit signage

Category street furniture
Type advertising sign

Category street furniture
Type fence

Category street furniture
Type road sign

Category street furniture
Type sign

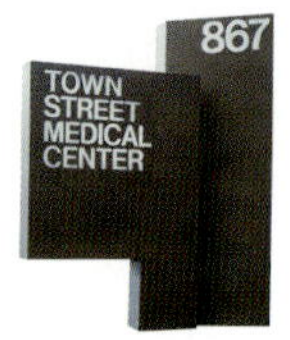

Category street furniture
Type bench

Category street furniture
Type bench

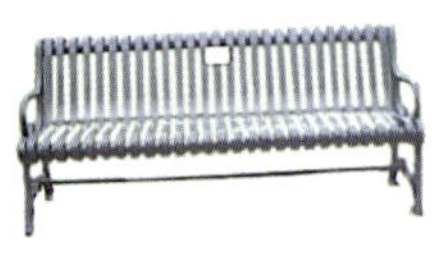

Category street furniture
Type public art

Category street furniture
Type fire hydrant

Category street furniture
Type newspaper dispensers

Category street furniture
Type street sign

Category street furniture
Type street sign

Category street furniture
Type planter

Category street furniture
Type parking sign

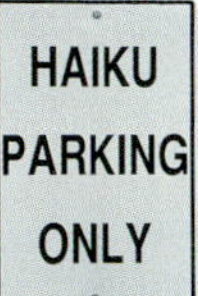

Category street furniture
Type street sign

Category street furniture
Type garbage bin

Category street furniture
Type trash can

Category street furniture
Type trash can

Category street furniture
Type bench

Category street furniture
Type traffic light

Category street furniture
Type phone booth

Category street furniture
Type advertising sign

Category street furniture
Type traffic cone

Category street furniture
Type gas pump

Category street furniture
Type bench

Category street furniture
Type planter

Category street furniture
Type playground equipment

Category street furniture
Type dumpster

Category **street furniture**
Type **portapotty**

Category **street furniture**
Type **street light**

Category **street furniture**
Type **street sign**

Category **street furniture**
Type **construction barricade**

Category **street furniture**
Type **playground equipment**

Category **street furniture**
Type **phone booth**

Category **street furniture**
Type **parking meter**

Category **street furniture**
Type **clock**

Category **street furniture**
Type **street light**

Category **street furniture**
Type **mailbox**

Category **street furniture**
Type **road sign**

Category **street furniture**
Type **playground equipment**

Category **street furniture**
Type **bench**

Category **street furniture**
Type **playground equipment**

Category **street furniture**
Type **sign**

Category **street furniture**
Type **playground equipment**

Category **street furniture**
Type **staircase**

Category **street furniture**
Type **topiary sculpture**

Category **street furniture**
Type **decoration**

Category **street furniture**
Type **vending machine**

Category **street furniture**
Type **newspaper dispensers**

Category **street furniture**
Type **street sign**

Category **street furniture**
Type **playground equipment**

Category **street furniture**
Type **rack**

Category **street furniture**
Type **gravestone**

Category **street furniture**
Type **bottles**

Category **street furniture**
Type **sign**

Category **street furniture**
Type **octopus**

Category **street furniture**
Type **bench**

Category **street furniture**
Type **bench**

In alphabetical order

Blackburn Recreation Center
263 Carpenter Street

Boys & Girls Clubs Westside Unit
115 South Gift Street

City of Columbus Police Impound Lot
400 W. Whittier Street

City of Columbus Traffic Management Center
109 North Front Street

Columbus Zoo
9990 Riverside Drive

COTA Administrative Offices and Bus Facility
1600 McKinley Avenue

Dodge Skatepark
667 Sullivant Avenue

Franklinton Cemetery
Souder Avenue at River Street

Franklinton Library
1061 W. Town Street

Franklin Park and Franklin Park Conservatory
1777 East Broad Street

German Village Meeting House
588 South 3rd Street

Greater Columbus Arts Council
100 East Broad Street, Suite 2250

Jim Arter's garden
1424 Bryden Road

The King Arts Complex
867 Mount Vernon Avenue

North Market
59 Spruce Street

Sawyer Recreation Center
1056 Atcheson Street

The Topiary Garden
E. Town St. & Washington Avenue

Volunteers of America
379 W. Broad Street

Wexner Center for the Arts
The Ohio State University
1871 North High Street

Project concept
Jeanne van Heeswijk
Curator
Carlos Basualdo
Co-curator
Steven Hunt
Project coordinator
Kelly Merryman

Participants
See inside front cover

The Interactor
Development and realization
V2_Lab, International Lab for
the Unstable Media,
Rotterdam, The Netherlands.
Concept Jeanne van
Heeswijk, Maaike Engelen
Software development Marco
Christis (Blixem Media)
© copyright V2_Lab

The Interactor team
Creative programmer
Marco Christis, Blixem Media
Interaction design
Enric Gili
Management V2_Lab
Anne Nigten
Interaction design intern
Bram Perry
Interface design
Lenno Verhoog
Sound design
Dave Hemmingway
Project management
Angela Verschelling

Education
Cynthia Collins, Kendra
Girardot, Chris Hutchins,
and the Wexner Center
education staff
Maaike Engelen
Children of the Future staff
Jim Arter, Tim Katz
Children of the Future artist
members (Thanks for their
generous collaboration day in
and day out during the nine
weeks of the project.)
Christina Gussler,
Gina Fiorino, Rob Jones,
Molly Lambert, Stephen
Mainard, Linda Miller,
Jeff Ostrowski, Michelle
Porreca, Kim Rhyan,
and Bob Silver

The Bus
Bus stop design
Atelier van Lieshout
Bus wrap
JB Squared Incorporated
COTA staff
Ron Barnes, Jim Daley,
Erica Franklin, Jackie Hill,
Tim Jansen, Cheryl
Lockhart, Trent Martin,
Kenneth Rawls, Jessica
Rubinstein, Pat Stevens,
Belinda Taylor, Roger
Vance, Don Wayt, Rich
Wood, Steve Yuszka,
and all the *Face Your World*
bus drivers
Interior bus design
Matt Clausen
Technical team
David Bamber, Larry "Pug"
Heller, Stephen Jones, Paul
Jones, Benjamin Knepper,
James A. Scott, John A.
Smith, Mike Sullivan, and
Microsoft's Mike Greer

Printed material
Text editor
Ann Bremner
Graphic design
Roger Teeuwen
Design assistance
Karin Lecarpentier
Photography
Rolf Engelen
Thanks to Darnell Lautt,
Jeffrey M Packard,
Myung Jin Song, and
Patricia Trumps

Web site
Created by V2_Lab
Interaction design and
program Bram Perry
Graphic design
Roger Teeuwen,
Lenno Verhoog

Film/DVD
Amanda Ault, Paul Hill,
Bill Horrigan, Jennifer Lange,
Martin Lucas

Special thanks to Mónica
Amor, Corina Crosetti,
Jill Davis, Craig Dransfield,
Okwui Enwezor, Wapke
Feenstra, Alicia Framis,
Nancy and Dave Gill,
François Xavier Guillon,
Carsten Höller, Hella
Jongerius, Sandra Licorish,
Sherri Trayser, Lucas
Verweij, and Dré Wapenaar
for their continuing support.
The project team expresses
appreciation to all the staff at
the Wexner Center for the
Arts for their creative
contributions in the
realization of this project.
Additional thanks go to all the
staff at COTA and at the
Greater Columbus Arts
Council and its Children of
the Future program, as well
as to Jill Bennett, Rich
Cunningham, Raymond
Humphrey, Ron Williams,
and their colleagues at
Blackburn Recreation
Center, the Boys & Girls
Clubs of Columbus
Westside Unit, and Sawyer
Recreation Center. Finally,
curator Carlos Basualdo
adds a note of particular
gratitude to Jeanne van
Heeswijk, Steven Hunt,
and Kelly Merryman for
their dedication to the project
and their friendship.

Face Your World was organized by the Wexner Center for the Arts in collaboration with the Greater Columbus Arts Council's Children of the Future program and COTA.

The artist's residency was presented with major support from the Greater Columbus Arts Council.

Major in-kind support was provided by the Greater Columbus Arts Council's Children of the Future program and COTA.

Additional support was provided by the Mondriaan Foundation, Amsterdam; the Consulate General of the Netherlands in New York; and the Corporate Annual Fund of the Wexner Center Foundation.

Special thanks to The City of Columbus, Recreation and Parks Department and the Boys & Girls Clubs of Columbus, Inc. for providing programming sites.

COLOPHON, COPYRIGHT, AND BOOK CREDITS

Published in association with
Notations
Face Your World
Jeanne van Heeswijk

Project concept
Jeanne van Heeswijk
Curator
Carlos Basualdo
Co-curator
Steven Hunt

Columbus, Ohio
June 17–August 16, 2002

Organized by the Wexner Center for the Arts, **The Ohio State University**, in collaboration with the **Greater Columbus Arts Council's Children of the Future program** and **COTA**.

Editor
Carlos Basualdo
Copy Editor
Ann Bremner
Graphic Design
Roger Teeuwen
Lithography
Marc Gijzen
Printer
Die Keure, Bruges, Belgium

Image Credits
Every effort has been made to obtain proper credit information and permission to reproduce images. All images not listed below are the work of Jeanne van Heeswijk, Rolf Engelen, or the participating children or are credited on the pages where they appear.
p.32 Bob Goedewaagen, Peter Cox;
p.33 Bob Goedewaagen;
p.36 Sakurai Tadahisa;
p.42 Bob Goedewaagen;
p.53 Amy Plant;
p.114 Matt Clausen;
p.115 Roger Teeuwen;
p.118 Kelly Merryman;
p.120 John Dearstyne.

Published by
Artimo
Fokke Simonszstraat 8
1017 TG Amsterdam
Netherlands
Tel: +31-20-330 2511
Fax: +31-20-330 2512
info@artimo.net
www.lostart.nl

Wexner Center for the Arts
The Ohio State University
1871 North High Street
Columbus, Ohio 43210-1393
USA
Tel: +1 614-292-0330
Fax: +1 614-292-3369
www.wexarts.org

ISBN:
90-75380-55-0

Distributed by
D.A.P.
155 Sixth Avenue, 2nd floor
NY 10013 New York
Tel: +1 212 627 1999
Fax: +1 212 627 9484
dap@dapinc.com

Idea Books
Nieuwe Herengracht 11
1011 RK Amsterdam
Tel: +31 20 622 6154
Fax: +31 20 620 9299
idea@ideabooks.nl

© 2002 Artimo and The Ohio State University, Wexner Center for the Arts; and the artists.

www.faceyourworld.net